Contents

Encourage Your Child to Develop a Growth Mindset

The research of psychologist Dr. Carol Dweck tells us that people have two possible mindsets—a fixed mindset or a growth mindset. People with a fixed mindset believe that they are either smart or good at something, or they are not—and nothing can change that. People with a growth mindset believe that it is always possible to get better at doing something. Dr. Dweck has found that students with a growth mindset are more motivated to learn and achieve more than students with a fixed mindset.

How can you help your child develop a growth mindset?

Talk about the brain. Explain that the brain becomes stronger by working hard to master new skills. Just as exercise makes muscles stronger, working at challenging thinking tasks makes the brain stronger.

View mistakes as learning opportunities. Let your child know that mistakes are valuable ways of learning where the problems lie. By carefully looking at mistakes, you and your child can learn where there are misunderstandings or missing pieces of knowledge. Mistakes pave the way to success!

Teach ways of dealing with frustration. Children can "turn off" when they become frustrated, which makes learning impossible. Teach your child ways to overcome frustration. For example, use the Internet to learn about breathing techniques that combat stress. You can also remind your child of skills that he or she mastered in the past (such as learning to tie shoelaces) that took time and effort to learn.

Focus on praising the process. While it's fine to praise your child or the results he or she achieved, you can encourage a growth mindset by focusing your praise on the process. For example, praise your child's willingness to keep trying and his or her use of effective learning strategies, such as asking questions.

Model a growth mindset. Look for opportunities to reinforce with your child how to see things from a growth mindset. For example:

If your child says…	Respond by saying…
I'll never get this!	Maybe you can't do it yet, but you'll get better if you keep trying.
I've been working at this for a long time and I'm still not getting it right.	Look at these areas where you've made progress. Keep working and you'll make more progress.
Hey, I can finally do this!	Let's think about how you achieved success. Some of the things you did this time might help you with the next challenge.

MONDAY • Sentences and Punctuation

1. A *sentence* expresses a complete thought. Circle the complete sentence. Underline the sentence fragment.

   a) Going to the store.   **b)** We need to go to the store.

2. The *complete subject* contains all the words that tell who or what the sentence is about. Circle the complete subject.

   a) The green garden snake slithered into the shade under a rock.

   b) The new couch in the family room folds out into a bed.

3. The *complete predicate* includes the verb and all the words that tell about what happened in the sentence. Underline the complete predicate.

   a) The colourful fall leaves tumbled and twirled in the wind.

   b) Two young children chased after the blue and white ball.

TUESDAY • Grammar and Usage

1. *Common nouns* name <u>non-specific</u> people, places, and things.
   Proper nouns name <u>specific</u> people, places, and things.

   Common nouns: girl   country   movie

   Proper nouns: Amanda   Mexico   The Lion King

   Circle the common nouns and underline the proper nouns.

   Most tourists love Rome, which is the largest city in Italy.

2. **Use the correct pronoun—*I* or *me*—to complete the sentence.**

   Elizabeth and _____ are going to an art exhibition at the museum.

3. **Circle the correct verb in brackets.**

   a) My father and sister (has   have) freckles.

   b) The soccer team (is   are) practising hard before the playoffs.

WEDNESDAY • Figures of Speech

1. Fill in the definitions using the words *literal* and *figurative*.

_____ language means exactly what it says. _____ language is a word or phrase that does not have its normal, everyday, literal meaning.

2. *Alliteration* is when two or more words in a phrase or sentence start with the same sound.

Example: "Please pass the pepper," Peter pleaded.

Underline the letters or sounds that repeat.

a) Ingrid is an innovator inspired by intelligent individuals.

b) Five fabulous flamingos finished eating their favourite food.

3. An *analogy* compares two things that seem different from each other but which have something in common. *Example: light = dark   as   cold = hot*

Write the missing word to complete the analogy.

banana = yellow   as   broccoli = _____

THURSDAY • Vocabulary and Spelling

A *root* or *base* word is a word that has a *prefix* or *suffix* added to it.

Base word	With prefix *pre*	With suffix *ing*
heat	preheat	heating

1. Identify and write the *base* word.

a) affordable _____   b) immature _____

c) discomfort _____   d) collection _____

2. A *synonym* is a word that means the same as another word.
Circle the synonym for the bolded word.

a) allow   sum up   permit   **b) split**   divide   connect

3. An *antonym* is a word that has the opposite meaning to another.
Circle the antonym for the bolded word.

a) artificial   homemade   natural   **b) common**   normal   rare

FRIDAY • Writing Prompt

A *proverb* is a saying that offers some advice on how to live your life.

1. a) Explain what you think the proverb below means. Draw the proverb.

"Strike while the iron is hot."

_____

_____

b) Can you think of a situation where someone should strike while the iron is hot? Give details.

_____

_____

_____

_____

_____

_____

☐ I checked for correct spelling.   ☐ I organized my ideas in a way that makes sense.

☐ I checked for correct punctuation.   ☐ I used linking words to connect my ideas.

☐ I used interesting words.   ☐ Challenge: I used a figure of speech.

MONDAY • Sentences and Punctuation

A *declarative* sentence is a *statement*. It ends with a period. (.)

An *interrogative* sentence is a *question*. It ends with a question mark. (?)

An *imperative* sentence is a *command* that tells someone to do something. It can end with a period or with an exclamation mark. (.) (!)

An *exclamation* is a sentence that *shows strong feeling* such as excitement, joy, or anger. It ends with an exclamation mark. (!)

1. Write the correct punctuation mark at the end of each sentence.

   a) Get ready for dinner _____   **b)** Can I help you _____

   c) I am from Canada _____   **d)** I so excited _____

2. A conjunction is a word that joins two sentences or ideas.
   Write the correct conjunction—*and*, *but*, or *for*.

   The house was now empty, _____ the previous owner had moved away.

TUESDAY • Grammar and Usage

1. **Circle the correct word in brackets.**

   The two (teams team's teams') captains provided excellent leadership.

2. A *transitive verb* is an action verb that needs a *direct object*. The direct object is something or someone who receives the action of the verb.

   Example: Miguel threw the baseball.

   The noun "baseball" is the direct object of the action verb "throw."

   In each sentence, underline the transitive verb and circle the direct object.

   a) Peter carefully brushes his teeth.   **b)** Jenna showed photos of her vacation.

3. **Circle the prepositions in each sentence.**

   a) The restaurant beside the lake is the best restaurant in town.

   b) The path goes between two large trees and then along the river.

WEDNESDAY • Figures of Speech

1. Underline the examples of alliteration in this sentence.

Come clean your cluttered closet.

2. Create an alliterative phrase using the word *shark*.

_____

3. *Similes* are phrases that use the words *as* or *like* to describe something or someone.

Examples: That old dog is as blind as a bat.   That test was as easy as ABC!

Does the sentence contain a simile? Circle YES or NO. Underline the simile.

a) Casey felt like a fish out of water.   **YES   NO**

b) Sana twirled her hair as she talked.   **YES   NO**

THURSDAY • Vocabulary and Spelling

1. A *homophone* is a word which sounds like another word, but which has a different spelling and meaning.

a) My favourite _____ are lilies.   (flower flour)

b) You need two cups of _____ for the cookie recipe. (flower   flour)

2. Underline the silent letter or letters in the words.

knapsack   thumb   gnome   wrist   knot

3. Circle the correct word to complete the sentence.

The walk to the village was (farther   farthest) than she thought.

4. Replace the underlined word with a synonym.

This is a very <u>comfortable</u> sofa. _____

FRIDAY • Writing Prompt

A *recount* tells about events in the order that they happened.
Write a recount of participating at a special event.

_____

_____

_____

_____

_____

_____

_____

_____

_____

_____

_____

_____

_____

_____

☐ I told the order of events using words like first, next, then, before, after, and finally.

☐ I ordered my ideas in a way that makes sense.

☐ I used "I" or "we" in my writing.

☐ I made sure to include details that answer who, what, where, when, and why.

☐ I checked for correct spelling and punctuation.

MONDAY • Sentences and Punctuation

1. Write a sentence about one of your favourite activities using each sentence type.

Declarative: _____

Interrogative: _____

Imperative: _____

Exclamation: _____

2. Write the correct conjunction—_for_, _so_, or _yet_.

The janitor said he washed the floor, _____ it still looks dirty.

3. Use a comma between the day and the year in a date.

My grandfather's birthday is July 7 1945.

TUESDAY • Grammar and Usage

1. An _antecedent_ is the word or words a pronoun refers to.

Example: The <u>thunderstorm</u> was severe, but **it** did not last long.

The noun "thunderstorm" is the antecedent of the pronoun "it."

Circle the antecedent of the underlined pronoun.

a) When Aunt Mary comes to town, we'll take <u>her</u> out for dinner.

b) Kevin is usually quite friendly, but today <u>he</u> seems to be in a bad mood.

2. Use the correct auxiliary (helping) verb below to complete the sentences.

could   may   might   must   should

a) _____ you please help me move these heavy boxes?

b) The juice has been in the fridge overnight, so it _____ be cold.

WEDNESDAY • Figures of Speech

1. *Hyperboles* are extreme exaggerations used for emphasis and for humour.

   Examples: Josh is so stuffed, he might explode!

   Underline the hyperbole in the sentence.

   Mimi jumped twenty metres when her cousin scared her from behind!

2. **Fill in the blank using a hyperbole.**

   June must have had _____ candles on her birthday cake!

3. a) **Underline the simile in the sentence.**

   Gary felt like a fish out of water at the meeting.

   b) **Explain the meaning.**

   _____

THURSDAY • Vocabulary and Spelling

1. **An *abbreviation* is the short form of a word and ends with a period. Write the abbreviation for each word.**

   a) Monday _____   b) December _____   c) Road _____

2. **Complete the sentence by writing *to, two,* or *too*.**

   I have _____ tickets _____ Tuesday's concert.

3. **Make the nouns plural by adding *s*. Add *es* to nouns that end with *s, x, ch*, or *sh*.**

   a) box _____   b) dish _____   c) bunch _____

4. **Use the word list to make four compound words.**

   craft   time   fire   body   air   life   place   any

   _____

FRIDAY • Writing Prompt

A *procedure* is a set of numbered steps to follow to make or do something. Write instructions that will clearly and accurately teach others to complete a task of your choice.

Description

_____

Materials or Ingredients

_____

_____

_____

Instructions

_____

_____

_____

_____

_____

_____

_____

_____

☐ I have a description that tells what you will make or do.

☐ The information is organized under headings.

☐ I used sequence words such as first, next, then, and last.

☐ I used action words to tell which actions to do.

☐ I checked for correct spelling and punctuation.

MONDAY • Sentences and Punctuation

A *compound sentence* contains two or more simple sentences. Each simple sentence in a compound sentence is called a *main clause*. A main clause contains a subject and a predicate.

Example: Alex laughed, but Joe did not like the joke.

A *complex sentence* has one *main clause* and one or more *subordinate clauses*. Subordinate clauses cannot stand alone.

Example: In the morning, I always have breakfast.

1. Identify the sentence as a compound or complex sentence.

a) I like sleeping in, but my brother likes to wake up early. _____

b) Before a piano recital, I practise piano each day. _____

TUESDAY • Grammar and Usage

1. Circle the correct word in brackets.

a) The (scientists scientist's scientists') discoveries won her several awards.

b) How many of the (workers worker's workers') voted to go on strike?

2. Complete each sentence with the correct relative pronoun.

who   whom   whose   which   that

a) The neighbour _____ car was stolen has bought a new one.

b) From his closet, Dad chose a tie _____ matched his blue eyes.

3. Choose the best word to fill in the blank.

a) _____ backpack is mine. (These This)

b) Our neighbours brought _____ cupcakes for us to all enjoy. (these this)

WEDNESDAY • Figures of Speech

A *metaphor* compares two things without using the words *like* or *as*.

Example: Her <u>eyes</u> were <u>fireflies</u>. "fireflies" means her eyes were twinkling in the dark.

1. Circle the two things being compared in each metaphor. Explain each metaphor.

   a) Sam is a rat for what he did to Amy.

   _____

   b) The backyard is a lake after all that rain.

   _____

**2. Rewrite the literal sentence to one that has figurative language.
Underline the figurative language.**

   July is a hot month. _____

THURSDAY • Vocabulary and Spelling

1. A *contraction* is one word made from two words, with one or more of the letters left out. The letters that are left out are replaced with an apostrophe.

   Write the contraction for each pair of words.

   a) I have _____ (I've   I'll)   **b)** you have _____ (you've   you'll)

2. Circle the best synonym for the underlined word below.

   Luke shows great <u>aptitude</u> for ski racing. He is trying out for the ski team.

   ability   interest

**3. Add a suffix to the base word in brackets so the sentence makes sense.
Sometimes, the new word is the past tense or present tense of the base word.**

   a) The handlebars on the bicycle were _____ . (adjust)

   b) Dan's new puppy Charlie is very _____ . (play)

FRIDAY • Writing Prompt

Persuasive writing gives your opinion and tries to convince the reader to agree with you.

Read the statement below. Write a persuasive paragraph to convince the reader of your opinion. Make sure to add details to support your ideas.

"People are too dependent on technology."

I (agree, disagree) that people are too dependent on technology.

First of all, _____

_____

_____

_____

Another reason _____

_____

_____

_____

Also, _____

_____

_____

_____

This is why I think _____

☐ I clearly stated my opinion.

☐ I stated strong reasons and gave details.

☐ I organized my ideas in a way that makes sense.

☐ I used linking words to connect my ideas.

☐ I checked for correct spelling and punctuation.

MONDAY • Sentences and Punctuation

1. **When the speaker tag comes *before* the spoken words, put a comma *after* the speaker tag before the first quotation marks.**

   Example: The man grumbled, "You've been no help at all."

   Add quotation marks. Add a comma if necessary.

   a) The waiter asked Would you like more water'?

   b) My sister complained That's not fair!

2. **Write the correct punctuation at the end of the sentence. Name the sentence type.**

   a) Do you know the time _____   _____

   b) Leave your boots here _____   _____

TUESDAY • Grammar and Usage

1. **Circle the common nouns and underline the proper nouns.**

   At City Centre Hospital, Dr. Patel waited for a patient to arrive by ambulance.

2. **Circle the prepositions in each sentence.**

   a) Across the street, I saw Dad waving at me.

   b) They looked into the deep well behind the old farmhouse.

3. **Circle the adverb that describes a verb.**
   Underline the verb that the adverb describes.

   a) Let's leave later so we can watch the movie.   **b)** The frightened deer ran away.

4. **Circle the correct word in brackets.**

   The (girl's girls' girls) tennis match takes place this afternoon.

WEDNESDAY • Figures of Speech

1. Finish the sentence using alliteration.

Five furry friends found _____

2. Finish the simile.

You look like a _____

3. Underline the hyperbole in the sentence.

Amanda cried a river of tears when her dog got lost.

4. Complete the analogies.

a) hot = cold   as   down =   **b)** ice = cold   as   fire =

5. Complete the hyperbole.

She is so lazy, she _____

THURSDAY • Vocabulary and Spelling

1. Fill in the blank with a synonym of the word in brackets.

a) Mission Control _____ the blastoff sequence. (started)

b) The _____ cupcakes were given out after the party. (surplus)

2. Make the nouns plural by adding s. For nouns that end with a consonant + y, change the y to an i and add es. For nouns that end with a vowel + y, just add s.

a) fly _____   **b)** valley _____   **c)** blackberry _____

d) baby_____   **e)** toy _____   **f)** decoy _____

3. The word *bow* has two meanings. Write two sentences to show each meaning.

_____

_____

FRIDAY • Writing Prompt

In an *acrostic* poem, the first letter of each line forms a word or phrase (vertically). An acrostic poem can describe the subject or even tell a brief story about it.

Example:

ALIENS

A lternative
L anding site
I n the dessert
E ast of the mountain range
N ear the solar panel array
S o be watching

Write an acrostic poem about a topic of your choice.

_____ _____

_____ _____

_____ _____

_____ _____

_____ _____

_____ _____

_____ _____

_____ _____

_____ _____

_____ _____

☐ I checked for correct spelling.   ☐ I organized my ideas in a way that makes sense.

☐ I checked for correct punctuation.   ☐ Challenge: I used a figure of speech.

☐ I used interesting words.

MONDAY • Sentences and Punctuation

1. When the speaker tag comes *after* the words someone says, put a comma *after* the last spoken word (before the final quotation mark). But *do not* add a comma if the spoken words end with a question mark or exclamation mark.

   Examples: "We'll all work together," the team leader said.   .

   Add quotation marks. Add a comma if necessary.

   a) It's time to go home said Mrs. Jackson.

   b) I think you're amazing! Rob told Jamal.

2. **Use a comma after *yes* or *no* when it appears at the beginning of a sentence.**

   a) Yes I followed the cookie recipe, but I also added some chocolate chips.

   a) No I prefer to walk to the store.

TUESDAY • Grammar and Usage

1. **Use the correct pronoun—*I* or *me*—to complete the sentences.**

   a) My friends and _____ love going to the movies on rainy Saturday afternoons.

   b) Ask Michelle or _____ to help you if you have any difficulties.

2. **A transitive verb is an action verb that needs a direct object.
   The direct object is something or someone who receives the action of the verb.**

   Example: The workers washed the windows.

   The noun "windows" is the direct object of the action verb "washed."

   In each sentence, underline the transitive verb and circle the direct object.

   a) The children sing songs around the campfire.

   b) The plumber bought supplies at the hardware store.

 Canadian Daily Language Skills, Grade 6   © Chalkboard Publishing Inc.

WEDNESDAY • Figures of Speech

1. An *oxymoron* is a pair of words that have opposite meanings placed side by side for effect.

   Examples: *pretty ugly*   *seriously funny*

   Underline the oxymoron in the sentence. Explain the meaning.

   The neighbour asked the children to keep the noise down to a dull roar.

   _____

2. Write a sentence for each example of an oxymoron above.

   _____

   _____

3. Underline the two things being compared in this metaphor.

   My life is nothing but a dream.

THURSDAY • Vocabulary and Spelling

1. Identify the word pair as synonyms or antonyms.

   a) capable, skilled _____

   b) brave, cowardly _____

2. Make the nouns plural. For some nouns that end with *o*, add *es*. For other nouns that end with *o*, just add *s*.

   a) piano _____   b) echo _____   c) potato _____

3. Fill in the blank with the correct word.

   I feel _____ about completing the bronze swim level.   (good well)

4. Write a sentence using another meaning of the underlined word.

   The children soon began to <u>tire</u> of the game and played something else.

   _____

FRIDAY • Writing Prompt

What does it mean to pick someone's brain? Is there anyone whose brain you would like to pick? Explain your reasons and give details.

_____

_____

_____

_____

_____

_____

_____

_____

_____

_____

_____

_____

_____

_____

_____

☐ I checked for correct spelling.   ☐ I organized my ideas in a way that makes sense.

☐ I checked for correct punctuation.   ☐ I used linking words to connect my ideas.

☐ I used interesting words.   ☐ Challenge: I used a figure of speech.

MONDAY • Sentences and Punctuation

1. **When the speaker tag comes in the middle of a spoken sentence, add a comma** *after* **the first group of spoken words and** *after* **the speaker tag.**

   Example: "I thought you might come," remarked Sam, "but I wasn't sure."

   Add the correct punctuation to the sentences.

   a) This clue said the detective is very interesting.

   b) Your conclusion said the teacher is based on strong evidence.

2. **If a sentence ends with a question, use a comma before the question.**

   Example: Tara watered the garden this morning, didn't she?

   Add commas where necessary in the sentences.

   a) The weather is cold for May isn't it?

   b) Our class has music after lunch don't we?

TUESDAY • Grammar and Usage

1. **Circle the correct word in brackets.**

   After the (birds   bird's   birds') wings had healed, it was able to fly again.

2. **A** *linking verb* **does** *not* **show action. A linking verb links the subject of a sentence to a noun or adjective in the predicate.**

   Example: The children were <u>excited</u> *today.*

   The verb "were" is a linking verb. In the sentence above, it links the subject ("The children") to an adjective ("excited").

   Fill in the circle beside the sentence if it contains a linking verb.

   a) O The dog buried a bone in the backyard.   **b)** O I am late for hockey practice.

3. **Write a sentence with a linking verb. Circle the linking verb.**

   _____

WEDNESDAY • Figures of Speech

1. *Onomatopoeia* **is the use of a word that sounds like what it names.**

Examples: brrr   sizzle   boing   pow

Circle the words in the list that are examples of onomatopoeia.

belch   chow   clunk   giggle   sleep   hum   screech   oink

2. Write a sentence using onomatopoeic words.

_____

3. Write a sentence using alliteration.

_____

5. Underline the hyperbole.

Marisa was dying to go the party.

THURSDAY • Vocabulary and Spelling

1. Underline the silent letter or letters in the words.

fudge   rhombus   scenic

2. Complete the sentence by writing *to* **or** *too.*

This soup is _____ hot _____ eat.

3. Make the nouns plural. For most nouns that end with *f,* **change the** *f* **to a** *v* **and add** *es.* **For a few nouns that end with** *f,* **just add the letter** *s.*

a) wife _____   **b)** cliff _____   **c)** shelf _____

4. Correct and rewrite the sentence.

Too peeple waited patiently to share there concerns with the principle.

_____

FRIDAY • Writing Prompt

Below is a saying that offers some advice on how to live your life.

1. a) Explain what you think the saying below means. Draw the saying.

"The grass is always greener on the other side."

_____

_____

b) Do you think this is a wise saying? Explain your thinking.

_____

_____

_____

_____

_____

☐ I checked for correct spelling.   ☐ I organized my ideas in a way that makes sense.

☐ I checked for correct punctuation.   ☐ I used linking words to connect my ideas.

☐ I used interesting words.   ☐ Challenge: I used a figure of speech.

MONDAY • Sentences and Punctuation

1. **When someone is speaking and says the name of the person he or she is speaking to, use a comma before and after the name.**

   Example: "By the way, Julian, I thought the speech you gave was excellent," I said.

   Add commas as necessary.

   a) "Angela could you please help me fold the laundry?" Mom asked.

   b) The children said, "You made a great dinner tonight Dad."

2. **Add the correct punctuation to the sentences.**

   a) I'll give you one more chance   the boss told Henry.

   b) Why did I do that I asked myself.

3. **Read the sentence. Circle the complete subject. Underline the complete predicate.**

   Fluffy white clouds drifted across the sky.

TUESDAY • Grammar and Usage

1. **An *antecedent* is the word or words a pronoun refers to.**

   *Example: The students are in the library doing research for **their** reports.*

   The noun "students" is the antecedent of the pronoun "their."

   Circle the antecedent of the underlined pronoun.

   After the performance, the audience showed <u>its</u> appreciation by clapping loudly.

2. **Complete each sentence with the correct relative pronoun.**

   who   whom   whose   which   that

   a) To _____ did the judges give the first prize?

   b) The man _____ sold me this painting said it would increase in value.

3. **Use the correct auxiliary (helping) verb below to complete the sentence.**

   can   could   may   might   must   should   will   would

   The invitation says that the wedding ceremony _____ start at 1 p.m.

WEDNESDAY • Figures of Speech

1. *Personification* is giving human qualities or abilities to an animal or object.

   Example: At exactly 6:30 a.m., my alarm clock sprang to life.
   (Alarm clocks can't come alive.)

   a) Underline the animal or thing being personified in this sentence.

   b) Circle what it is doing to show that it is an example of personification.

   Lightning danced across the sky.

   c) Explain why it is personification.

   _____

2. **a) Underline the two things being compared in the metaphor.**
   b) Write your own version of the metaphor.

   The desert is heaven!

   The desert is _____

THURSDAY • Vocabulary and Spelling

1. **Fill in the blank with the correct homophone**

   a) The doctor has three _____ in the waiting room. (patience patients)

   b) Don't lose your _____ as you wait for your turn. (patience patients)

2. **Write the contraction for each pair of words.**

   a) they will _____ (they've they'll) **b)** we had _____ (we'd we've)

3. **Make the nouns plural.**

   a) wood _____ **b)** ratio _____ **c)** man _____

4. **How many syllables are there in the word participation?** _____

5. **Which is stronger? Circle the answer.** (scared petrified)

FRIDAY • Writing Prompt

Write a review that shares your opinions about a book, movie, restaurant, destination, a piece of technology, or something else of your choice.

This is a review of _____

Description _____

_____

Review _____

_____

_____

_____

_____

_____

_____

_____

_____

_____

_____

_____

☐ I hooked my readers with a strong sentence about my topic.

☐ I stated strong reasons and gave details.

☐ I organized my ideas in a way that makes sense.

☐ I used linking words to connect my ideas.

☐ I checked for correct spelling and punctuation.

MONDAY • Sentences and Punctuation

1. **When someone is speaking and says the name of the person they are speaking to, use a comma between the name and the rest of the sentence.**

   Example: "Chris, did you text me?" she asked. I replied, "Yes, I did, Sophie."

   Add the correct punctuation to the sentences below.

   a) Alexa you need to get ready for your appointment Mom said

   b) Maybe you could come too Carlos I suggested.

2. **Correct and rewrite the sentence.**

   for, lunch we had Burritos vegetable sticks and milk?

   _____

3. **Write an imperative sentence that includes a person's name and someone speaking.**

   _____

TUESDAY • Grammar and Usage

1. **Circle the correct word in brackets.**

   Some of this old (books book's books') pages are yellow and torn.

2. **Use the correct pronoun—*I* or *me*—to complete the sentences.**

   a) Jessica, Kurt, and _____ are working together on a Science Fair project.

   b) The actor said, "The award was given to my co-stars and _____ ."

3. **A *linking verb* does *not* show action. A linking verb links the subject of a sentence to a noun or adjective in the predicate.**

   *Example: I **am** <u>scared</u> of spiders.*

   The verb "am" is a linking verb. In the sentence above, it links the subject ("I") to an adjective ("scared").

   Fill in the circle beside the sentence if it contains a linking verb.

   a) ◯ My grandfather was a plumber.   **b)** ◯ A bulldozer pushed away the dirt.

WEDNESDAY • Figures of Speech

1. a) Underline the animal or thing being personified in this sentence.
b) Circle what it is doing to show that it is an example of personification.

The taxi cab was impatient as it waited for the passenger to get in.

c) Explain why it is personification.

_____

2. Circle the words in the list that are examples of onomatopoeia.

honk   rattle   dull   peep   clank   moo   whine   smack

3. Write a sentence using two of the onomatopoeic words from the list above.

_____

4. Write the missing word to complete the analogies.

a) fork = eat   as   cup = _____   **b)** boat = sail   as   car = _____

THURSDAY • Vocabulary and Spelling

1. Write the abbreviation for each word.

a) Saturday _____   **b)** Tuesday _____   **c)** Friday _____

2. Identify each pair of words as synonyms (S), antonyms (A), or homophones (H).

a) country, nation ____   **b)** past, present ____   **c) hour, our ____**

3. Fill in the blank with the correct word.

a) Please (accept except) my apologies!

b) I have piano lessons every Tuesday (accept except) on holidays.

4. Correct and rewrite the sentence.

Arent' theese read strawberrys delicious?

_____

FRIDAY • Writing Prompt

A *fact* is information that can be *proven* to be true. An *opinion* is a statement based on something a person *thinks* or *believes* to be true.

Fill in the table with two examples of facts and two examples of opinion.

Statement	Fact or Opinion	How do you know? Explain your thinking.

MONDAY • Sentences and Punctuation

1. **Identify whether the underlined part of the sentence is the complete subject or the complete predicate. Circle *CS* for the complete subject or *CP* for the complete predicate.**

   Mr. and Mrs. Ramirez <u>wait patiently for the rain to stop</u>. **CS   CP**

2. **Add the correct punctuation to the sentences below.**

   a) Please feel free to ask questions   said the guest speaker.

   b) When will the train leave   the young woman asked.

3. **Add commas to separate the items in a series.**

   Jupiter Saturn and Uranus are the largest planets in our solar system.

4. **Identify the sentence as a compound or complex sentence.**

   While I do homework, I sometime have music playing. _____

TUESDAY • Grammar and Usage

1. **Circle the common nouns and underline the proper nouns.**

   Tickets for shows at the Winchester Theatre are cheaper on Mondays.

2. **A transitive verb is an action verb that needs a direct object. The direct object is something or someone who receives the action of the verb.**

   Example: Angela collects stamps.

   The noun "stamps" is the direct object of the action verb "collects."

   Underline the transitive verb and circle the direct object.

   The goalie caught the puck in his glove.

3. **Circle the correct verb in brackets.**

   The fastest runner in all the races (was were) a girl in my class.

WEDNESDAY • Figures of Speech

1. *Idioms* are everyday phrases that mean something different from what they say. Even though the phrase doesn't make literal sense, people understand its meaning. Match each idiom to its correct meaning.

Idiom	Meaning
chew someone out	delicious
down to the wire	yell at someone
finger lickin' good	never will happen
when pigs fly	rushing to meet a deadline

2. **Fill in the blanks with onomatopoeic words.**

   a) Han noisily _____ his soup off his spoon.

   b) The corn flakes _____ loudly as Nora crushed them with a rolling pin.

3. **Write a simile using the word *as*.** _____

THURSDAY • Vocabulary and Spelling

1. **Circle the words that have the sound of *long a*. Underline the words that have the sound of *short a*.**

   integration   fair   dare   absolutely   actual   always   table

2. **Write the contraction for each pair of words.**

   a) does not _____ (doesn't don't)   **b)** are not _____ (aren't isn't)

3. **Write the plural form of the noun in brackets to complete the sentence.**

   I saw two _____ crossing the road.   (deer)

4. **How many syllables are there in the word *apostrophe*?** _____

5. **Determine the meaning of the underlined word.**

   The lady was <u>conspicuous</u> in her orange hat, purple coat, and green army boots.

   _____

FRIDAY • Writing Prompt

Persuasive writing gives your opinion and tries to convince the reader to agree with you.

Read the statement below. Write a persuasive paragraph to convince the reader of your opinion. Make sure to add details to support your opinion.

"I think people should be allowed to vote from the age of _____."

People should be allowed to have a cellphone from the age of _____.

_____

_____

_____

_____

_____

_____

_____

_____

_____

_____

This is why I think people should be allowed to have a cellphone from the age of _____.

☐ I clearly stated my opinion.

☐ I stated strong reasons and gave details.

☐ I organized my ideas in a way that makes sense.

☐ I used linking words to connect my ideas.

☐ I checked for correct spelling and punctuation.

MONDAY • Sentences and Punctuation

1. Write the correct punctuation at the end of the sentence. Name the sentence type.

Our family is moving to Cape Breton _____   _____

2. Read the sentence. Circle the complete subject. Underline the complete predicate.

A brown squirrel ran along the fence.

3. Write the correct conjunction—*but*, *for* or *so*.

This brochure is very informative, _____ we still have some questions.

4. Add the correct punctuation to the sentences below.

a) It's a good plan agreed Paul   but will it work

b) I think Angelo plays on the soccer team doesn't he

TUESDAY • Grammar and Usage

1. Circle the correct word in brackets.

a) The (printers printer's printers') blue ink cartridge had run out.

b) His new (TVs TV's TVs') remote control has so many buttons!

2. Complete each sentence with the correct relative pronoun.

who   whom   whose   which   that

"I would like to speak to the person _____ is in charge," he said.

3. Circle the prepositions in the sentence.

I signed my name on the birthday card for Aunt Selma.

4. Circle the adverb in the sentence that describes another adverb. Underline the adverb it is describing.

When the fire alarm rang, we walked very quickly out of the building.

WEDNESDAY • Figures of Speech

1. Use the idiom in the sentence to show its correct meaning.

down to the wire

_____

2. Complete the analogy.

a) bird = _____ as fox = den **b)** knee = leg as elbow = _____

3. Use the word list to finish each oxymoron.

big   good   opinion   words

a) unbiased _____ **b)** _____ baby

4. Rewrite the literal sentence to one that has figurative language. Underline the figurative language.

The room was silent. _____

THURSDAY • Vocabulary and Spelling

1. Fill in the blank with the correct word.

Megan had a fever and a stomachache. She felt _____ . (bad badly)

2. Identify the word pair as synonyms or antonyms.

a) frequent, seldom _____

b) gloomy, miserable _____

3. Circle the correct word.

a) I had practised for my speech, so I was (all ready already) to present.

b) The bus will be late because (it's its) engine had not been repaired.

4. What is the meaning of the underlined word?

I <u>implore</u> you to please help me. I am desperate. _____

FRIDAY • Writing Prompt

A *cinquain* is a poem that has five lines.

Use the lines below to write cinquain poems about a person, place, or thing.

FORMAT

Line 1: two syllables

Line 2: four syllables

Line 3: six syllables

Line 4: eight syllables

Line 5: two syllables

FORMAT

Line 1: two syllables

Line 2: four syllables

Line 3: six syllables

Line 4: eight syllables

Line 5: two syllables

☐ I used interesting words.   ☐ I checked for correct spelling and punctuation.

MONDAY • Sentences and Punctuation

1. Use a colon before giving a list of three or more items.

Example: I have three favourite fruits: apples, oranges, and grapes.

Add a colon to the sentence.

There are several items on my shopping list eggs, milk, bread, tea, and juice.

2. Add commas where necessary in the sentences.

a) Yes I am coming back later.   **b)** The volleyball game is at 2 o'clock isn't it?

3. Add quotation marks and commas to each sentence.

a) Minnie exclaimed   I didn't know your dog was having puppies!

b) Mrs. Stevens said in a welcoming voice   John please make yourself at home.

4. Write the correct conjunction—*but, for* or *so*.

The weather is extremely cold, _____ I will wear a sweater under my coat.

TUESDAY • Grammar and Usage

1. Circle the common nouns and underline the proper nouns.

"In April last year, the weather stayed cold all month," remarked Uncle Max.

2. Use the correct pronoun—*I* or *me*—to complete the sentences.

a) The teacher asked Karen and _____ to collect the test papers.

b) Sam and _____ collected donations for the food bank.

3. A linking verb does *not* show action. A linking verb links the subject of a sentence to a noun or adjective in the predicate.

*Example: My brother **feels** <u>sick</u> today.*

The verb "feels" is a linking verb in the sentence above. "Feels" links the subject ("My brother") to an adjective ("sick").

Fill in the circle beside the sentence if it contains a linking verb.

O The woman's perfume smelled nice.

WEDNESDAY • Figures of Speech

1. Use each idiom in a sentence to show its correct meaning.

finger lickin' good

_____

when pigs fly

_____

2. Use the idea to write a sentence using hyperbole.

sleeping in

_____

THURSDAY • Vocabulary and Spelling

1. Complete the sentences by writing their, there, or they're.

a) What is _____ last name?

b) Our volleyaball team keeps winning, because _____ practising each day.

c) _____ are six people assigned to each table.

2. Write three words that rhyme with *plane.*

_____

3. Rewrite the sentence using contractions and abbreviations.

Mister Tanaka cannot attend the meeting being held at 25 Beech Street.

_____

FRIDAY • Writing Prompt

A *proverb* is a saying that offers some advice on how to live your life.

1. a) Explain what you think the proverb below means. Draw the proverb.

"Don't bite tha hand that feeds you."

_____

_____

b) Do you think this is good advice? Explain your thinking.

_____

_____

_____

_____

_____

☐ I checked for correct spelling.   ☐ I organized my ideas in a way that makes sense.

☐ I checked for correct punctuation.   ☐ I used linking words to connect my ideas.

☐ I used interesting words.   ☐ Challenge: I used a figure of speech.

MONDAY • Sentences and Punctuation

1. **Use a colon before giving a list of three or more people or things.**

   The store had three flavours of yogurt   strawberry, blueberry, and vanilla.

2. **What is missing in the sentence fragment below? Circle the answer.**

   climbed the apple tree

   (who or what is doing the action   the action   both are missing)

3. **Rewrite the sentence fragment. Add what is missing to make a complete sentence.**

   _____

4. **Write an example of an exclamation that includes a speaker.**

   _____

TUESDAY • Grammar and Usage

1. **Circle the antecedent of the underlined pronoun.**

   My partner and I feel certain that <u>our</u> presentation will be the best.

2. **In each sentence, underline the action verb and circle the direct object.**

   a) Mr. Silverstein boils water to make tea.   **b)** The courier delivers the parcels promptly.

3. **Use the correct auxiliary (helping) verb below to complete the sentence.**

   can   could   might   must   will   would

   Dad said that when I was a baby, I _____ cry whenever I had a bath.

4. **Circle *ADJ* if the underlined word is used as an adjective.**
   Circle *N* if the underlined word is used as a noun.

   a) We watched the results of the election on the <u>morning</u> news.   *ADJ*   *N*

   b) We saw a report about the election on the news this <u>morning</u>.   *ADJ*   *N*

WEDNESDAY • Figures of Speech

1. **Underline the two things being compared in the metaphor.**

   a) Canada is a melting pot of different cultures.

   b) José is a worm for going behind Maria's back like that.

2. **Finish the hyperbole.**

   a) It's so hot you could _____ !

   b) It's so cold, I _____ !

3. **a) Underline the animal or thing being personified in this sentence.**
   b) Circle what it is doing to show that it is an example of personification.

   What little hope I had left walked right out the door.

   c) Explain why it is personification.

   _____

THURSDAY • Vocabulary and Spelling

1. **What is the meaning of the underlined word?**

   After hibernating all winter, the bear <u>emerged</u> from its cave.

   _____

2. **Underline the silent letter or letters in the words.**

   cologne   knight   rhythm

3. **In the blank, write an antonym for the word in brackets.**

   It was raining, so Kelly's dog _____ to go outside.   (agreed)

4. **Choose the best word to fill in the blank.**

   I was _____ tired _____ sleepy.   (neither   nor)

FRIDAY • Writing Prompt

People ask for advice when they have a problem or would like an opinion about something. Give advice to someone about a specific situation. Convince the person that your advice is worth taking by explaining your thinking.

Situation: _____

Dear _____ ,

_____

_____

_____

_____

_____

_____

_____

_____

_____

_____

Your friend, _____

☐ My ideas are clear and convincing.

☐ I checked for correct spelling and punctuation.

☐ Challenge: I used a figure of speech.

☐ I ordered my ideas in a way that makes sense.

MONDAY • Sentences and Punctuation

1. Write the correct conjunction—_for_, _nor_, or _or_.

The sick puppy did not eat, _____ did it want to play.

2. Identify the sentence as a compound or complex sentence.

Did you forget about the party, or did you decide not to come? _____

3. Change the statement to an imperative sentence and include a speaker.

Don't go outside in the rain.

_____

4. Correct and rewrite the sentence.

dinosaur provincial park in drumheller alberta is a popular tourist attraction?

_____

TUESDAY • Grammar and Usage

1. Circle the common nouns and underline the proper nouns.

People gathered on Parliament Hill in Ottawa to watch a display of fireworks.

2. Circle the correct pronoun in brackets for the antecedent in bold.

The **police** finally caught (its his their) suspect last Thursday.

3. Complete each sentence with the correct relative pronoun.
who   whom   whose   which   that

The woman _____ photo you took is a former astronaut.

4. A _phrase_ is a group of two or more words. A _prepositional phrase_ begins with a preposition.

_Example: The clock **_over_ the sink** is always slow._

Underline the prepositional phrase in the sentence below..

We saw many factories along the highway.

WEDNESDAY • Figures of Speech

1. Write a sentence using the idiom *a green thumb* to show its meaning.

_____

2. Complete the analogy.

Monday = day   as   November = _____

3. Use the oxymoron in a sentence to show its meaning.

big baby

_____

4. a) Underline the simile in the sentence.   The gymnast is as nimble as a monkey.

b) Explain the meaning.

_____

THURSDAY • Vocabulary and Spelling

1. Fill in the blank with the best word.

The developers _____ the old house, before rebuilding.
(ruined demolished)

2. Circle the correct word.

a) The miniter stood at the (alter   altar) and welcomed the parishioners.

b) Mom said she could (alter   altar) my dress in time for the dance.

3. Write the contraction for each pair of words.

a) they had _____ (they'll they'd)   **b)** we have _____ (we'd we've)

4. Determine the meaning of the underlined word in the sentence.

Mr. Chen <u>admonished</u> the children about the dangers of throwing snowballs at windows.

_____

FRIDAY • Writing Prompt

A *procedure* is a set of numbered steps to follow to make or do something. Write instructions that will clearly and accurately teach others to complete a task of your choice.

Description

_____

Materials or Ingredients

_____

_____

_____

Instructions

_____

_____

_____

_____

_____

_____

_____

☐ I have a description that tells what you will make or do.

☐ The information is organized under headings.

☐ I used sequence words such as first, next, then, and last.

☐ I used action words to tell which actions to do.

☐ I checked for correct spelling and punctuation.

MONDAY • Sentences and Punctuation

1. Identify the sentence as a compound or complex sentence.

Mike threw the ball and it went over the fence. _____

2. Add a colon and commas to the sentence as necessary.

These are the people on my team Wyatt Owen Sydney and Andrew.

3. Add the correct punctuation.

If you're busy said Rachel I could call you later.

4. Write the correct punctuation mark at the end of the sentence. Name the sentence type.

When is your guitar lesson _____   _____

5. Write an example of a declarative sentence.

_____

TUESDAY • Grammar and Usage

1. Fill in the circle beside the sentence if the underlined pronoun has an unclear antecedent.

a) O Sophia gave Mom <u>her</u> gloves.

b) O Mom passed <u>her</u> gloves to Sophia.

2. Circle the correct word in brackets.

a) The signatures on the (paintings   painting's   paintings') were hard to read.

b) The (dogs dog's dogs') collar has a tag with a number on it.

3. Circle the correct verb in brackets.

The owner of these skateboards (are is) willing to sell them.

4. Choose the best word to fill in the blank.

_____ bowl is full of fruit.   (These That)

WEDNESDAY • Figures of Speech

1. Below are some song lyrics and a movie title. Are they examples of onomatopoeia? Circle YES or NO.

a) "Zing went the strings of my heart"   **YES   NO**

b) "It went zip when it moved"   **YES   NO**

c) "The mouse takes the cheese"   **YES   NO**

2. Is this an example of alliteration? Circle YES or NO.

a) Sparky ran to the neighbour's yard and chased their cat.   **YES   NO**

b) Freddy figured finding fudge would be fun and fulfilling.   **YES   NO**

3. Underline the hyperbole in the sentence.

My grandfather's car is a hundred years old!

THURSDAY • Vocabulary and Spelling

1. Circle the word that is spelled correctly.

isno't   isn't   isnt'

2. Choose the correct word.

_____ people voted in the election this year.   (Fewer Less)

3. Circle the correct name of the competition in which athletes compete in three sports.

triathlon   multilevel   biathlon

4. Think of a synonym for the word in brackets. Write the word in the blank.

I go to the library _____ to get books to read.   (frequently)

FRIDAY • Writing Prompt

Persuasive writing gives your opinion and tries to convince the reader to agree with you.

Read the statement below. Write a persuasive paragraph to convince the reader of your opinion. Make sure to add details to support your opinion.

"The best superpower to have would be _____.**"**

_____

_____

_____

_____

_____

_____

_____

_____

_____

_____

_____

_____

_____

☐ I clearly stated my opinion.

☐ I stated strong reasons and gave details.

☐ I organized my ideas in a way that makes sense.

☐ I used linking words to connect my ideas.

☐ I checked for correct spelling and punctuation.

MONDAY • Sentences and Punctuation

1. Read the sentence. Circle the complete subject. Underline the complete predicate.

The passengers on the train showed their tickets to the conductor.

2. Identify the sentence as a compound or complex sentence.

Whenever I travel, I always bring an extra outfit.

3. Add the correct punctuation.

What a wonderful gift   exclaimed Roberto

4. Is this a run-on sentence? Circle YES or NO.

The bikes are in the driveway they need to be in the garage. _____

5. Write an example of an interrogative sentence.

_____

TUESDAY • Grammar and Usage

1. *Abstract* **nouns name ideas you cannot see or touch.**

Example: patience

Underline the abstract noun.

Rita was grateful for the kindness of the people who had helped her.

2. Use the correct pronoun—*I* **or** *me***—to complete the sentence.**

You could draw a portrait of Hakim or _____ for your art project.

3. Does the underlined linking verb link the subject to a noun or an adjective? Write "noun" or "adjective" beside each sentence.

a) The audience <u>seemed</u> bored by the play. _____

b) I <u>am</u> a detective with the city police. _____

Canadian Daily Language Skills, Grade 6   © Chalkboard Publishing Inc.

WEDNESDAY • Figures of Speech

1. Underline the onomatopoeic words in the sentence.

Tommy heard the zip, zap, zoom of the toy race car.

2. Write a sentence that includes onomatopoeic words.

_____

3. a) Underline the animal or thing being personified in this sentence.
b) Circle what it is doing to show that it is an example of personification.

The rain gave me pecks on the cheek as it fell from the sky.

c) Explain why it is personification.

_____

4. Write a sentence that includes a figure of speech. Identify the figure of speech.

_____

THURSDAY • Vocabulary and Spelling

1. Circle the correct word to complete the sentence.

The pink rose had the sweetest _____.   (cent   scent)

2. Write the contraction for each pair of words.

a) I had _____ (I've I'd)   **b)** you have _____ (you've you'll)

3. Make the nouns plural.

a) sandwich _____   **b)** burrito _____

c) ox _____   **d)** mouse _____

4. What is the meaning of the underlined word?

Gloria's migraine headache was <u>debilitating</u>. She couldn't do anything all day.

_____

FRIDAY • Writing Prompt

A *Diamond* poem is a poem that makes the shape of a diamond.

Choose a person, place, or thing and write a Diamond poem using nouns, verbs and adjectives.

_____
a one-word noun

_____   _____
an adjective that describes   an adjective that describes
the noun   the noun

_____   _____   _____
a verb that ends in "ing" and   a verb that ends in "ing" and   a verb that ends in "ing" and
describes the noun   describes the noun   describes the noun

_____   _____   _____   _____
a second noun that relates   a second noun that relates   a second noun that relates   a second noun that relates
to the first noun   to the first noun   to the first noun   to the first noun

_____   _____   _____
a verb that ends with "ing"   a verb that ends with "ing"   a verb that ends with "ing"

_____   _____
an adjective   an adjective

_____
a third noun

☐ I used interesting words.   ☐ I checked for correct spelling and punctuation.

          Canadian Daily Language Skills, Grade 6   © Chalkboard Publishing Inc.

MONDAY • Sentences and Punctuation

1. **Identify whether the underlined part of each sentence is the complete subject or the complete predicate. Circle *CS* for the complete subject or *CP* for the complete predicate.**

   <u>The willow trees in the backyard</u> swayed back and forth in the wind.   ***CS   CP***

2. **Fill in the blank with the best conjunction.**

   I was walking to the skating arena _____ it started to snow.   (since   when)

3. **Add quotations and other punctuation as necessary.**

   When I was a little girl said Grandma we walked a mile to school every day

4. **Write the correct punctuation at the end of the sentence. Name the sentence type.**

   Watch out _____   _____

TUESDAY • Grammar and Usage

1. **Circle the correct pronoun in brackets for the antecedent in bold.**

   a) A **snake** sheds (his her its) skin as it grows.

   b) The **explorers** were tired after the long journey, so (it them they) rested for a week before returning home.

2. **In each sentence, underline the transitive (action) and circle the direct object.**

   a) Leo checks his answers on the test.

   b) Yolanda inserted paper into the printer.

3. **Circle the prepositions in each sentence.**

   a) Through the window, Mario saw a woman walking with two children.

   b) There are some interesting antiques in the store beside the park.

WEDNESDAY • Figures of Speech

1. *Onomatopoeia* is the use of a word that sounds like what it names.
Think of something that says:

   a) Hoot! _____   **b)** Creak! _____

2. **Use the oxymoron in a sentence to show its meaning.**

   inside out

   _____

3. **a) Underline the simile in the sentence.**   Melinda eats like a bird.

   b) Explain the meaning.

   _____

4. **Write a silly sentence using alliteration.**

   _____

THURSDAY • Vocabulary and Spelling

1. **Write the contraction for each pair of words.**

   a) she had _____ (she'd   she'll)   **b)** he will _____ (he'll   he'd)

2. **What is a word that has three syllables?** _____

3. **Write the homophones for the words in brackets.**

   I can _____ with both my left hand and my _____ .   (right   write)

4. **Choose the best word to fill in the blank.**

   I saw _____ Carlos _____ Tina at recess.   (neither   nor)

5. **Order the words from general to specific.**

   _____ dessert   _____ cake   _____ food

FRIDAY • Writing Prompt

Do you think you could go without using the internet for a month? Explain your thinking.

_____

_____

_____

_____

_____

_____

_____

_____

_____

_____

_____

_____

_____

_____

☐ I checked for correct spelling.

☐ I checked for correct punctuation.

☐ I used interesting words.

☐ I organized my ideas in a way that makes sense.

☐ I used linking words to connect my ideas.

☐ Challenge: I used a figure of speech.

MONDAY • Sentences and Punctuation

1. What is missing in the sentence fragment below? Circle the answer.

went to bed early

(who or what is doing the action   the action   both are missing)

2. Rewrite the sentence fragment. Add what is missing to make a complete sentence.

_____

3. Write the correct conjunction—_or, so,_ or _yet_.

It was nearly midnight, _____ we were not sleepy at all.

4. Correct and rewrite the sentence.

"we've eaten, at this restaurant before haven't we? asked Leo."

_____

TUESDAY • Grammar and Usage

1. Circle the antecedent of the underlined pronoun.

The teacher said to Tina, "With a little more effort, <u>you</u> could get better marks."

2. Complete the sentence with the correct relative pronoun.

who whom whose which that

The person _____ wrote that song is a musical genius.

3. Use the correct auxiliary (helping) verb to complete the sentence.

can may must should will would

My baby brother Mark _____ grow up to be as tall as our father.

WEDNESDAY • Figures of Speech

1. a) Underline the idiom in the sentence.

Harry had to buckle down and study for his test.

b) Explain the meaning.

_____

2. Is this an example of alliteration? Circle YES or NO.

a) Bob the baker burned both the bread and the buns.   **YES   NO**

b) The mice will play when the cat is away.   **YES   NO**

3. Complete the analogy.   feet = _____   as   hands = fingers

4. Use the idea to write a sentence using hyperbole.   lifting something heavy

_____

THURSDAY • Vocabulary and Spelling

1. The letters _ee_, _ea_, _ie_, and _ey_ can make the long e sound you hear in _deer_. Fill in the blank to spell each word correctly.

a) Wipe your t_____rs away.   **b)** I lost my house k_____s.

c) In spring we plant s_____ds.   **d)** May I have a p_____ce of pie?

2. Write the correct plural for the noun in brackets.

The _____ made delicious foods for the mayor's party.   (chef)

3. Correct and rewrite the sentence.

Their are ten familys who live on our streat.

_____

FRIDAY • Writing Prompt

A *proverb* is a saying that offers some advice on how to live your life.

1. a) Explain what you think the proverb below means. Draw the proverb.

"The pen is mightier than the sword."

_____

_____

b) Do you think this is a wise saying? Explain your thinking.

_____

_____

_____

_____

☐ I checked for correct spelling.   ☐ I organized my ideas in a way that makes sense.

☐ I checked for correct punctuation.   ☐ I used linking words to connect my ideas.

☐ I used interesting words.   ☐ Challenge: I used a figure of speech.

MONDAY • Sentences and Punctuation

1. **Write the correct conjunction—_for, nor,_ or _or_.**

   The sick puppy did not eat, _____ did it want to play.

2. **Add quotation marks and any other punctuation required.**

   May I help you? asked the salesperson.

3. **Identify the sentence as a compound or complex sentence.**

   I forgot about baseball practice until my mom reminded me.

4. **Change the declarative sentence to an imperative sentence.**

   I am going _____

5. **Write a sentence that includes items in a series.**

   _____

TUESDAY • Grammar and Usage

1. **Fill in the circle beside the sentence if the underlined pronoun has an unclear antecedent.**

   a) O I provided reasons for my conclusions, but <u>they</u> aren't very clear.

   b) O Mrs. Shultz told her neighbour that <u>her</u> dog got out of the yard.

2. **Use the correct pronoun—_I_ or _me_—to complete the sentence.**

   The little puppy looked up at my parents and _____ with sad eyes.

3. **Circle the correct verb in brackets.**

   a) My brother or my sister (has have) played a trick on me!

   b) My grandparents (has have) been going to Florida every winter for years.

WEDNESDAY • Figures of Speech

1. a) Underline the oxymoron in the sentence. .

The parents kept a close distance from the children as they played on the climbers.

b) Explain the meaning of the oxymoron

_____

2. Underline the two things being compared in the metaphor.

My toes are ice cubes.

3. Rewrite the sentence by adding onomatopoeic words.

_____

4. Replace the phrase in the brackets with a hyperbole.

My dinner is (too hot) _____

THURSDAY • Vocabulary and Spelling

1. Write the abbreviation for each word.

a) Avenue _____   **b)** Mister _____   **c)** Quebec _____

2. In each sentence, underline the pair of synonyms, antonyms, or homophones. Then circle S for synonyms, A for antonyms, or H for homophones.

a) Dan said the beginning of the story was okay, but it came to an odd conclusion.
   S A H

b) The woman filled the pail with flowers in bright and pale colours.   **S A H**

3. Fill in the blank with the correct word.

That was a _____ good milkshake. (real really)

4. What is a word that has four syllables? _____

FRIDAY • Writing Prompt

A *recount* tells about events in the order that they happened.
Write a recount of an event of your choice.

_____

_____

_____

_____

_____

_____

_____

_____

_____

_____

_____

_____

☐ I told the order of events using words like first, next, then, before, after, and finally.

☐ I ordered my ideas in a way that makes sense.

☐ I used "I" or "we" in my writing.

☐ I made sure to include details that answer who, what, where, when, and why.

☐ I checked for correct spelling and punctuation.

MONDAY • Sentences and Punctuation

1. Read the sentence. Circle the complete subject. Underline the complete predicate.

The house with the black roof caught fire last week.

2. Write the correct punctuation at the end of the sentence. Name the sentence type.

This is the funniest movie I have ever seen _____   _____

3. Add a colon and commas to the sentence as necessary.

The animals at the zoo include mammals reptiles birds and amphibians.

4. Correct and rewrite the sentence.

i can't wait to visit, Stanley Park in Vancouver British Colombia?

_____

TUESDAY • Grammar and Usage

1. Circle the common nouns and underline the proper nouns.

Last Friday at City Hall, the mayor answered questions from reporters.

2. Circle the correct pronoun in brackets for the antecedent in bold.

This scientist has made some important **discoveries**, but she did not receive credit for (it them they).

3. Does the underlined linking verb link the subject to a noun or an adjective? Write "noun" or "adjective" beside the sentence.

The students will <u>be</u> interested in this topic. _____

WEDNESDAY • Figures of Speech

1. Use the idiom in a sentence to show its correct meaning.

wrong side of the bed.

_____

2. Identify two types of figures of speech in the sentence.

The sizzling bacon jumped out the pan and onto my plate.

a) _____

b) _____

3. Underline the two things being compared in the metaphor.

a) Bruno's temper was a volcano.   **b)** Hannah's bedroom is a zoo with all her pets.

THURSDAY • Vocabulary and Spelling

1. Underline the silent letter or letters in the words.

rhapsody   wedge   enough

2. What is the abbreviation for the month you were born? _____

3. Circle the contraction in each sentence. Write the words that form the contraction.

a) I've had a great time at the birthday party. _____

b) They're going miniature golfing on Friday night _____

4. Write the correct plural for the noun in brackets.

a) Many _____ lined up early for the store sale.   (person)

b) I went fishing and caught six _____ .   (trout)

FRIDAY • Writing Prompt

A *procedure* is a set of numbered steps to follow to make or do something.
Write the recipe for your favourite snack or dessert.

Description

_____

Materials or Ingredients

_____

_____

_____

Instructions

_____

_____

_____

_____

_____

_____

_____

☐ I have a description that tells what you will make or do.

☐ The information is organized under headings.

☐ I used sequence word such as first, next, then, and last.

☐ I used action words to tell which actions to do.

☐ I checked for correct spelling and punctuation.

MONDAY • Sentences and Punctuation

1. **Complete each sentence with the correct conjunction—_but_, _for_, or _so_.**

   a) Jason tiptoed down the hall _____ no one would hear him.

   b) Mr. Russo wants to take a vacation, _____ he is much too busy.

2. **Add quotation marks and any other punctuation required.**

   I have the flu explained Kim so I can't come.

3. **Unscramble these words to make a sentence that is an exclamation.**

   the best I ever pizza this is eaten have

   _____

4. **Add commas as necessary to the sentence.**

   Riding a bike walking to school and playing sports are all good exercise.

TUESDAY • Grammar and Usage

1. **Fill in the circle beside the sentence if the underlined pronoun has an unclear antecedent.**

   a) O Mr. Lee told his nephew that <u>he</u> had artistic talent.

   b) O We didn't pick many apples from the tree because <u>they</u> weren't ripe yet.

2. **In each sentence, underline the transitive (action) verb and circle the direct object.**

   a) The storm broke a large branch off the tree.

   b) The Johnsons often cook steaks on their barbecue.

3. **Circle _ADJ_ if the underlined word is used as an adjective. Circle _N_ if the underlined word is used as a noun.**

   a) My favourite <u>vegetable</u> is broccoli.   **ADJ   N**

   b) Have you tried the <u>vegetable</u> soup at the cafeteria?   **ADJ   N**

WEDNESDAY • Figures of Speech

1. Use the idiom *out of the blue* in a sentence to show its correct meaning.

_____

2. Identify two types of figures of speech in this sentence.

The clanging of the pots and pans woke up the whole city!

_____

3. a) Underline the two things being compared in the metaphor.

Opportunity was knocking at her door.

b) Explain the meaning of the metaphor.

_____

4. Use the oxymoron *open secret* in a sentence to show its meaning.

_____

THURSDAY • Vocabulary and Spelling

1. Circle the correct word to complete the sentence.

Your health is (more   most) important than money.

2. Write the contraction for each pair of words.

a) she will _____ (she'd   she'll)   **b)** he had _____ (he'll   he'd)

3. Complete the spelling of each word using the letters *ti* or *ci*.

a) sugges____on   **b)** magi____an   **c)** cau____ous

4. What is the meaning of the underlined word?

After working all day and not eating, Carlos was <u>ravenous</u>.

_____

5. Write a word with four syllables. _____

FRIDAY • Writing Prompt

Persuasive writing gives your opinion and tries to convince the reader to agree with you.

Read the statement below. Write a persuasive paragraph to convince the reader of your argument. Make sure to add details to support your opinion.

"The school day should start later and finish earlier."

I (agree, disagree) that the school day should start later and finish earlier.

_____

_____

_____

_____

_____

_____

_____

_____

_____

_____

_____

_____

_____

☐ I clearly stated my opinion.

☐ I stated strong reasons and gave details.

☐ I organized my ideas in a way that makes sense.

☐ I used linking words to connect my ideas.

☐ I checked for correct spelling and punctuation.

MONDAY • Sentences and Punctuation

1. Is this a run-on sentence? Circle YES or NO?

I dried the dishes and my sister put the dishes away.   **YES   NO**

2. Add the correct punctuation to the sentence.

I am very proud of you said Grandma Sophia I can see you have worked hard

3. Write an example of a compound sentence.

_____

4. Rewrite the sentence using correct capitalization and punctuation.

my friends and i shared some milk cookies and apple slices!

_____

TUESDAY • Grammar and Usage

1. Underline the pronoun whose antecedent is the noun in bold.

The **students** take care not to break the test tubes as they wash them.

2. Circle the correct word in brackets.

The (politicians politician's politicians') supporters helped her get elected.

3. Use the correct auxiliary (helping) verb to complete the sentence.

can   may   will   would

a) Because my broken leg healed well, I _____ dance again.

b) It is June, so I am certain the weather _____ get warmer soon.

4. Complete the sentence with the correct relative noun.

who   whom   whose   which   that

The woman _____ wallet I returned called to thank me.

WEDNESDAY • Figures of Speech

1. a) Underline what is being personified in the sentence.
b) Circle what is happening to show that it is an example of personification.

The turkey dinner didn't agree with Jack's stomach.

c) Explain why it is personification.

_____

2. Use the idea to write a sentence using onomatopoeic words.

eating spaghetti

_____

3. Write a sentence with alliteration using the letter _S_.

_____

THURSDAY • Vocabulary and Spelling

1. Write the correct plural for the noun in brackets.

a) The _____ howled at the moon.   (wolf)

b) The beef _____ were delicious!   (burrito)

2. Write the contraction for each pair of words.

a) could not _____   (couldn't   can't)

b) would not _____   (won't   wouldn't)

3. Think of a synonym for the word in brackets. Write the word in the blank.

The dog fell into the mud puddle by _____ . (mishap)

4. Correct the spelling of each word.

a) busyest _____   **b)** stoped _____

FRIDAY • Writing Prompt

Draw a picture and write the text for a missing object or pet.

MISSING

Who or What? _____

When? _____ Where? _____

Description _____

_____

_____

_____

_____

_____

_____

Contact _____ Reward _____

☐ My writing makes sense.   ☐ I used descriptive words and phrases.

☐ My picture is neat and colourful.   ☐ I checked for correct spelling
                                           and punctuation.

MONDAY • Sentences and Punctuation

1. Fill in the blank with the correct conjunction.

We had a bite to eat _____ we got home.   (as soon as   while)

2. Add quotation marks and any other punctuation required.

The child whispered I know the answer to the secret

3. What is missing in the sentence fragment below? Circle the answer.

cleaned the house from top to bottom.

(who or what is doing the action   the action   both are missing)

4. Rewrite the sentence fragment.
Add what is missing to make a complete sentence.

_____

TUESDAY • Grammar and Usage

1. Abstract nouns name ideas you cannot see or touch.   *Example: misery*
Underline the abstract nouns.

Brave soldiers displayed their patriotism by fighting for freedom.

2. Complete each sentence with the correct relative pronoun.

who   whom   whose   which   that

a) That boy _____ you dislike so much is actually quite nice.

b) Jupiter, _____ is the largest planet in our solar system, is the fifth planet
from the Sun.

3. Circle the correct verb in brackets.

a) Jan and Roberta sometimes (stop stops) by for a quick visit.

b) The choir (has have) been giving free concerts all summer long.

WEDNESDAY • Figures of Speech

1. What does the oxymoron *working vacation* mean?

_____

2. Complete the analogies.

a) shoe = foot   as   hand = _____

b) tall = short   as   wide = _____

3. Use the idea to write a sentence using hyperbole.

listening to loud music

_____

4. Underline and identify the figure of speech in the sentence.

Her entire day screeched to a halt. _____

THURSDAY • Vocabulary and Spelling

1. In the sentence, underline the pairs of synonyms, antonyms, or homophones. Then circle S for synonyms, A for antonyms, or H for homophones.

a) Trevor carefully picked up the fragile decoration, which was extremely delicate. **S A H**

b) Glen got spooked at the creek because the old tree's branches creak. **S A H**

2. Write the contraction for each pair of words.

a) she will _____ (she'd she'll)   b) he had _____ (he'll he'd)

3. Choose the best word to complete the sentence.

I find the (more most) interesting things when I clean out my closet.

4. Correct the sentence for spelling mistakes. Rewrite the sentence.

I saw sum beautiful butterflys fllying around the patioes.

_____

FRIDAY • Writing Prompt

If you could live anywhere, where would that be? Give details.

_____

_____

_____

_____

_____

_____

_____

_____

_____

_____

_____

_____

☐ I checked for correct spelling.   ☐ I organized my ideas in a way that makes sense.

☐ I checked for correct punctuation.   ☐ I used linking words to connect my ideas.

☐ I used interesting words.   ☐ Challenge: I used a figure of speech.

MONDAY • Sentences and Punctuation

1. **Read the sentence. Circle the complete subject. Underline the complete predicate.**

   The loud construction outside woke me up early this morning.

2. **Write the correct punctuation at the end of each sentence. Name the sentence type.**

   I am feeling tired _____   _____

3. **Write the correct conjunction—_for_, _so_, or _yet_.**

   She was tired when she got home, _____ she had been walking all day.

4. **Correct and rewrite the sentence.**

   felix go to mexican delight and pick up tortilla chips salsa and burritos   said Dad

   _____

TUESDAY • Grammar and Usage

1. **Circle the correct pronoun in brackets for the antecedent in bold.**

   Jeff could not clearly see the blades of the old airplane's **propeller** until (it them they) stopped spinning.

2. **Use the correct pronoun—_I_ or _me_—to complete the sentences.**

   Angry bees swarmed all around my dog and _____.

3. **Fill in the circle beside the sentence if it contains a linking verb.**

   a) O Two young children played quietly in the sandbox.

   b) O The crumbling old bridge seemed unsafe.

WEDNESDAY • Figures of Speech

1. Write a silly sentence using alliteration and a simile.

_____

2. a) Underline the oxymoron in the sentence.

The directions to the house I got from Luke were clear as mud!

b) Explain the meaning.

_____

3. Read the sentence. Identify the figure of speech.

a) The hinges complained loudly as the door opened slowly. _____

b) Concert is to noisy as library is to quiet. _____

c) That's a monster snow cone! _____

THURSDAY • Vocabulary and Spelling

1. Write the abbreviation for each word.

a) January _____   **b)** litre _____   **c)** tablespoon _____

2. What is the meaning of the underlined word?

I need to drink more milk; my doctor says my diet is <u>deficient</u> in calcium.

_____

3. Complete the spelling of each word using the letters *ti* or *ci*.

a) gra____ous   **b)** audi____on   **c)** fa____al

4. Choose the correct word to complete the sentence.

This office building is the (older oldest) in the city.

FRIDAY • Writing Prompt

Create a new expression that people can use as advice in their daily lives. Draw and write about the saying.

1. a) **What is your new saying?**

_____

   b) **Explain what it means.**

_____

_____

   c) **How can this new saying relate to a person's daily life?**

_____

_____

_____

_____

_____

☐ I checked for correct spelling.   ☐ I organized my ideas in a way that makes sense.

☐ I checked for correct punctuation.   ☐ I used linking words to connect my ideas.

☐ I used interesting words.   ☐ Challenge: I used a figure of speech.

MONDAY • Sentences and Punctuation

1. Write an example of a complex sentence.

_____

2. Add quotation marks and any other punctuation required.

Get out of my way! yelled the driver   I'm in a hurry

3. Write the correct conjunction—_for_, _so_, or _yet_.

I don't remember ever meeting that woman before, _____ she looks familiar.

4. Rewrite the sentence using correct capitalization and punctuation.

glen is it true that st patrick's day is morgan s favourite holiday!

_____

TUESDAY • Grammar and Usage

1. Fill in the circle beside the sentence if the underlined pronoun has an unclear antecedent.

a) O Take the radio out of the box and then give <u>it</u> to me.

b) O If you have information about these events, you should share <u>it</u>.

2. Does the underlined linking verb link the subject to a noun or an adjective? Write "noun" or "adjective" beside the sentence.

I hope to <u>become</u> captain of my hockey team. _____

3. Circle the prepositions.

I read a book about space travel by a former astronaut.

WEDNESDAY • Figures of Speech

1. a) Underline what is being personified in the sentence.
   b) Circle what is happening to show that it is an example of personification.

   When she read the rejection letter for her novel, her dreams of becoming a writer died.

   c) Explain why it is personification.

   _____

2. Use the oxymoron *incredibly dull* in a sentence to show its meaning.

   _____

3. Use the onomatopoeic words *splish* and *splosh* in a sentence.

   _____

4. Read the sentence. Identify the figure of speech.

   The spicy chilli was fireworks in my mouth. _____

THURSDAY • Vocabulary and Spelling

1. Circle the words that have the sound of *long i*.
   Underline the words that have the sound of *short i*.

   island   impress   majority   dice   listen   high

2. Identify each pair of words as synonyms (S), antonyms (A), or homophones (H).

   a) deep, shallow _____   **b)** him, hymn _____

   c) forget, remember _____   **d)** achieve, attain _____

3. In the blank, write an antonym for the word in brackets.

   a) The item wasn't what he ordered, so Hadi _____ to pay
   for it.   (agreed)

   b) George added a very _____ stamp to his collection.
                                    (common)

FRIDAY • Writing Prompt

A *recount* tells about events in the order that they happened.
Write a recount of an event of your choice.

_____

_____

_____

_____

_____

_____

_____

_____

_____

_____

_____

_____

_____

☐ I clearly stated my opinion.

☐ I stated strong reasons and gave details.

☐ I organized my ideas in a way that makes sense.

☐ I used linking words to connect my ideas.

☐ I checked for correct spelling and punctuation.

MONDAY • Sentences and Punctuation

1. Which sentence is correct? Put a check mark beside the correct sentence.

a) He exclaimed, "A huge fish jumped out of the water and scared me!" _____

b) "He exclaimed," A huge fish jumped out of the water and scared me! _____

2. Add quotation marks and commas as necessary.

a) The waiter asked Would you like more water?

b) Please hand in your papers   said the teacher.

3. Change the interrogative sentence to an exclamation.

Who knows where the car is parked?

_____

TUESDAY • Grammar and Usage

1. Circle the correct word in brackets.

The (carpets carpet's carpets') in all the hallways were stained and dusty.

2. Underline the transitive (action) verb and circle the direct object.

a) At the circus, a seal balanced a ball on its nose.

b) Dad carries the suitcases out to the car.

3. A *phrase* is a group of two or more words. A *prepositional phrase* begins with a preposition.

*Example: The muffins **<u>from</u> Adele's Bakery** are delicious!*

Underline the prepositional phrase.

The picnic tables by the lake have just been painted.

WEDNESDAY • Figures of Speech

1. Use the idiom in a sentence to show its correct meaning.

with flying colours

_____

2. Write a silly sentence using alliteration.

_____

3. a) Underline the two things being compared in the metaphor.

All the world's a stage.

b) Explain the meaning of the metaphor.

_____

THURSDAY • Vocabulary and Spelling

1. Underline the silent letter or letters in the words.

receipt   assign   climb

2. Write the contraction for each pair of words.

a) is not _____ (it's isn't)   **b)** it is _____ (its it's)

3. Write the plural form of each noun.

a) body _____   **b)** moss _____   **c)** hunch _____

4. Identify each pair of words as synonyms (S), antonyms (A), or homophones (H).

a) aim, purpose _____   **b)** aloud, allowed _____   **c)** early, late _____

5. Choose the correct word to complete the sentence.

What is the (worse worst) thing that can happen?

FRIDAY • Writing Prompt

A *procedure* is a set of numbered steps to follow to make or do something. Write a procedure.

Description

_____

Materials or Ingredients

_____

_____

_____

Instructions

_____

_____

_____

_____

_____

_____

_____

_____

☐ I have a description that tells what you will make or do.

☐ The information is organized under headings.

☐ I used sequence words such as first, next, then, and last.

☐ I used action words to tell which actions to do.

☐ I checked for correct spelling and punctuation.

MONDAY • Sentences and Punctuation

1. **Identify whether the underlined part of each sentence is the complete subject or the complete predicate. Circle *CS* for the complete subject or *CP* for the complete predicate.**

   a) <u>The big toe of my left foot</u> is sore today. **CS   CP**

   b) A girl in my classroom <u>can also speak two other languages</u>. **CS   CP**

2. **Write the correct punctuation at the end of the sentence. Name the sentence type.**

   This bug bite really stings ____   _____

3. **Add the correct punctuation to the sentence.**

   For this weather said Dad you need a warm coat.

4. **Write the correct conjunction—*or, so,* or *yet*.**

   The scientist wanted to confirm his results, _____ he repeated the experiment.

TUESDAY • Grammar and Usage

1. **Underline the pronoun whose antecedent is the noun in bold.**

   a) **Fire** was destroying the forest, but firefighters said they couldn't stop it.

   b) The teacher asked the **students** several questions, and they did not have trouble answering them.

2. **Complete each sentence with the correct relative pronoun.**

   who   whom   whose   which   that

   a) The police are looking for the person _____ footprints were found at the scene of the crime.

   b) We're going to a concert featuring the singer _____ I told you about.

3. **Use the correct auxiliary (helping) verb to complete the sentences.**

   can   might   must   should

   I'll call Barb to see if she _____ be able to come over earlier.

WEDNESDAY • Figures of Speech

1. Read the sentence. Identify the figure of speech.

a) The dishes fell to floor with a loud crash and clatter.

_____

b) Actor is to movie as clown is to circus.

_____

2. Use the idea to write a sentence with hyperbole.

being late

_____

3. Write your own example of personification.

_____

THURSDAY • Vocabulary and Spelling

1. Circle the contraction that uses the apostrophe correctly.

aren't   arenot'   are' not

2. Choose the correct word to complete the sentence.

The mermaid was the (happier happiest) when playing in the sea.

3. Fill in the blank with the correct word.

The situation was going from _____ to _____ . (bad worse)

4. Write a new sentence using an antonym for the underlined word.

The <u>problem</u> was that the plumbing system needed repair.

_____

FRIDAY • Writing Prompt

Design a restaurant menu! First, choose foods for your menu. Then, write a detailed description for each menu item. Use interesting words to make customers' mouths water!

Restaurant Name

_____

Starters

_____

_____

_____

Main Courses

_____

_____

_____

_____

Dessert Specials

_____

_____

_____

Drinks

_____

_____

☐ My writing makes sense.

☐ My descriptions will make people want to order the food.

☐ I checked for correct spelling and punctuation.

MONDAY • Sentences and Punctuation

1. Insert quotation marks and the correct punctuation.

Raj ate lunch with his sister   said Tobi   and I ate with Sanjay

2. Read the sentence. Circle the complete subject. Underline the complete predicate.

That part of the movie was so funny that I laughed out loud.

3. Fill in the blank with the correct conjunction.

I picked up some extra groceries _____ I was already at the store. (since   when)

4. What is missing in the sentence fragment below? Circle the answer.

jumped for joy

(who or what is doing the action   the action   both are missing)

TUESDAY • Grammar and Usage

1. Abstract nouns name ideas you cannot see or touch.

Example: courage

Underline the abstract nouns.

Since his childhood, he had felt compassion for homeless people.

2. Fill in the circle beside the sentence if the underlined pronoun has an unclear antecedent.

a) O If you have questions for the guest speakers, you should ask <u>them</u>.

b) O Mom and Dad told the woman that <u>she</u> looked familiar.

3. Circle the correct verb in brackets.

José or Samuel (was were) going to help me paint my front porch.

WEDNESDAY • Figures of Speech

1. Read the sentence. Identify the figure of speech.

a) The frost painted beautiful pictures on the windows. _____

b) My mom says my room is a disaster area! _____

2. Rewrite the sentence to include onomatopoeic words.

Hc ran up thc mountain.

_____

3. Write a silly sentence using alliteration.

_____

4. Make up your own sentence using personification. Explain your thinking.

_____

THURSDAY • Vocabulary and Spelling

1. Write the contraction for each pair of words.

a) can not _____ (don't can't)

b) will not _____ (won't wouldn't)

2. Choose the correct word to complete the sentence.

Larry is the (better best) basketball player on the team.

3. Write the plural form of each noun.

a) house _____   **b)** chorus _____

4. What is the meaning of the underlined word?

Let me know if anything is <u>lacking</u> from what I owe you.

_____

FRIDAY • Writing Prompt

Haiku is a traditional style of Japanese poetry. Usually, haiku poems have a nature theme, such as animals or the seasons. Haiku poems are a good way to describe something.

Haiku poems have only three lines. There are five syllables in its first line, seven syllables in its second line, and five syllables in its third line. The third line is usually a subject that is only slightly connected to the first two lines.

Example: Leaves blow in the wind
                 Skies darken and thunder booms.
                 The rain helps things grow.

1. Write your own haiku. Choose a subject for your haiku. Brainstorm a list of words about your subject. Beside each word, note how many syllables it has.

2. Choose a second subject for the last line of your haiku. It should remind the reader of the subject.

3. Write your haiku.

Line 1 (5 syllables) _____

Line 2 (7 syllables) _____

Line 3 (5 syllables) _____

MONDAY • Sentences and Punctuation

1. Write the correct punctuation at the end of the sentence. Name the sentence type.

It is supposed to be cold and rainy tomorrow ____   _____

2. Identify the sentence as compound or complex.

My neighbour called an ambulance and it arrived quickly. _____

3. Insert quotation marks and the correct punctuation.

I don't understand this math   exclaimed Carlos   Can you please help me

4. Identify whether the underlined part of the sentence is the complete subject or the complete predicate. Circle *CS* for the complete subject and *CP* for the complete predicate.

That afternoon the children <u>attended a play at the Grand Theatre</u>.   *CS*   *CP*

TUESDAY • Grammar and Usage

1. Circle the correct pronoun in brackets for the antecedent in bold.

a) **Kittens** do not open (its   there   their) eyes until seven to ten days after birth.

b) The park's **garden** is full of lovely flowers, but unfortunately (it   them   they) is also full of weeds.

2. Fill in the circle beside the sentence if it contains a linking verb.

a) ○   Scientists are fascinated by this new species of frog.

b) ○   The police investigated a break-in at the electronics store.

3. A phrase is a group of two or more words. A prepositional phrase begins with a preposition.

*Example: The people **of our city** have elected a new mayor.*

Underline the prepositional phrase in each sentence.

The flowers under the shady tree do not get much sun.

WEDNESDAY • Figures of Speech

1. Read the sentence. Identify the figure of speech.

   a) Max is proud as a peacock about winning a trophy. _____

   b) When she heard those words, her happy mood died. _____

2. Finish the sentence with hyperbole.

   I'm so excited about my birthday! _____

3. Create your own analogy.

   _____

4. Rewrite the sentence to include a simile.

   The garden was beautiful.

   _____

THURSDAY • Vocabulary and Spelling

1. Complete the sentence by writing *their*, *there,* or *they're.*

   _____ are ten students going from our school to the presentation.

2. Choose the correct word to fill in the blank.

   The _____ (do dew) on the grass soaked my _____ . (feet feat)

3. Write the plural form of each noun.

   a) window _____   **b)** mix _____   **c)** battery _____

4. Write the contraction for each pair of words.

   a) has not _____ (hasn't hadn't)   **b)** must not _____ (mustn't must've)

5. Fill in the blank with any, *some,* or *no*.   (any   some)

   We'd like _____ juice. Is there _____?

FRIDAY • Writing Prompt

Who is someone you admire? Give your reasons.

_____

_____

_____

_____

_____

_____

_____

_____

_____

_____

_____

_____

☐ I clearly stated my opinion.

☐ I stated strong reasons and gave details.

☐ I organized my ideas in a way that makes sense.

☐ I used linking words to connect my ideas.

☐ I checked for correct spelling and punctuation.

MONDAY • Sentences and Punctuation

1. Write the correct conjunction—*for*, *nor*, or *or*.

I can make you a sandwich, _____ would you prefer soup and a salad?

2. Add commas as necessary.

The teacher gave us each some paper a pencil and an eraser for the test.

3. Correct and rewrite the sentence.

Dave asked Did "you find the book you were looking for, Jayce"!

_____

4. Write an example of a compound sentence.

_____

TUESDAY • Grammar and Usage

1. Fill in the circle beside the sentence if the underlined pronoun has an unclear antecedent.

a) O If you're too warm with a sweater under your coat, take <u>it</u> off.

b) O Joan told Helen that no one would believe <u>her</u>.

2. Circle the prepositions in each sentence.

a) I received an email from Uncle George with photos attached to it.

b) Vera sat between her two friends on the bench.

**3. Circle *ADJ* if the underlined word is used as an adjective.
Circle *N* if the underlined word is used as a noun.**

a) Sometimes I get dropped of at my mom's <u>office</u>.   *ADJ*   *N*

b) The <u>office</u> building has thirty floors.   *ADJ*   *N*

WEDNESDAY • Figures of Speech

1. Read the sentence. Identify the figure of speech.

a) It will take me a million years to finish this project! _____

b) Hopefully Henry's home has heat. _____

c) The company was in a state of constant change. _____

2. Write a silly sentence using alliteration.

_____

3. Use the idiom in a sentence to show its correct meaning.

to butter up someone

_____

THURSDAY • Vocabulary and Spelling

1. The word in brackets is marked as a synonym (S), an antonym (A), or a homophone (H) for the missing word. Write the correct word in the blank.

Sandy was very sick and her skin was _____ .   (pail; **H**)

**2. Circle the words that have the sound of *long o.*
Underline the words that have the sound of *short o.***

known   fold   dolphin   rolling   most   toast   smog   modal   got

3. Write the contraction for each pair of words.

a) do not _____ (don't can't)

b) will not _____ (won't we'd)

4. Choose the best word to complete the sentence.

Jill acts _____ politely when there are adults around.   (more most)

FRIDAY • Writing Prompt

A *fact* is information that can be *proven* to be true. An *opinion* is a statement based on something a person *thinks* or *believes* to be true.

Fill in the table with two examples of facts and two examples of opinion.

Statement	Fact or Opinion	How do you know? Explain your thinking.

MONDAY • Sentences and Punctuation

1. Read the sentence. Circle the complete subject. Underline the complete predicate.

The pilot flew the plane right across three provinces.

2. Fill in the blank with the best conjunction.

My friend needs to go home soon _____ it's time for dinner.

(after   because)

3. Add commas as necessary.

Gigi and her family live in Charlottetown Prince Edward Island.

4. Correct and rewrite the sentence.

I "said we're going to the Mall   said mya"   but "we're really taking her to the zoo"?

_____

TUESDAY • Grammar and Usage

1. Use the correct pronoun—*I* or *me*—to complete the sentences.

a) The delivery person had parcels for both my brother and _____.

b) "Tell your dad or _____ if you are going to be late," Mom said.

2. In each sentence, underline the transitive (action) verb and circle the direct object.

a) On the elevator, we pressed the button for the top floor.

b) Our neighbours painted their fence bright yellow.

3. Decide whether the underlined word is used as an adjective or adverb.

Jana went <u>straight</u> home after soccer practice.

WEDNESDAY • Figures of Speech

1. Make up your own sentence using personification. Explain your thinking.

_____

_____

2. a) Underline the simile in the sentence.

John's stomach rumbled like thunder.

b) Explain the meaning.

_____

3. Read the sentence. Identify the figure of speech.

The avalanche devoured everything in its path. _____

THURSDAY • Vocabulary and Spelling

1. Complete the sentence by writing _to, two_ or _too_.

Our _____ cousins coming with us _____ the ski hill.

2. Identify and write the base word.

a) uncontrollable _____

b) incorrectly _____

3. Circle the correct word.

a) A backpack will _____ the strain on your arms.　(lesson　lessen)

b) I have a piano _____ every Thursday.　(lessen　lesson)

4. Order the words from general to specific.

sentence _____ paragraph _____ word _____

FRIDAY • Writing Prompt

Write a letter to your future self.

_____
DATE

Dear _____,
GREETING

BODY

_____

_____

_____

_____

_____

_____

_____

_____

_____

_____

_____

_____

_____

Sincerely, _____
CLOSING / SIGNATURE

☐ I checked for spelling and punctuation. ☐ I ordered my ideas in a way that makes sense.

MONDAY • Sentences and Punctuation

1. Write the correct punctuation at the end of the sentence. Name the sentence type.

Ouch, that really hurts ____   _____

2. Correct and rewrite the sentence.

Judy Whined   dad said I have to clean my room this weekend?

_____

3. Correct the run-on sentence.

The dog chased the squirrel the squirrel ran away.

_____

4. Write a sentence that includes a series and is an interrogative sentence.

_____

TUESDAY • Grammar and Usage

1. Circle the correct pronoun in brackets for the antecedent in bold.

a) This **company** is very proud of the quality of (its their there) products.

b) A new office tower is being built across from the condo where my **grandparents** live, and we expect that it will spoil (its our their) view.

2. Use the correct auxiliary (helping) verb to complete the sentences.
can may must would

a) The weather forecast says snow _____ begin to fall around noon.

b) Now that I have glasses, I _____ see much more clearly.

3. Circle the correct verb in brackets.

a) My parents (has have) often asked me to be more responsible.

b) Neither Michael nor Frank (want wants) to wash the smelly trash bins.

WEDNESDAY • Figures of Speech

1. **What does the idiom *where there is smoke there is fire* mean?**

   _____

2. **Read each sentence. Identify the figure of speech.**

   a) I watched that new movie last night. It's a new classic! _____

   b) The novel was so popular, it flew off the shelves. _____

3. **Write an example of a sentence that includes alliteration and a simile.**

   _____

4. **Replace the word in the brackets with a hyperbole.**

   The hotel is (big) _____

THURSDAY • Vocabulary and Spelling

1. **Write the plural form of each noun.**

   a) store _____   **b)** flamingo _____

2. **Write the contraction for each pair of words.**

   a) does not _____ (doesn't don't)   **b)** are not _____ (aren't isn't)

3. **In the sentence, underline the pair of synonyms, antonyms, or homophones. Then circle S for synonyms, A for antonyms, or H for homophones.**

   I heard there's a dairy farm over the hill that has a large herd of cows. **S   A   H**

4. **What is the meaning of the underlined word?**

   Sam felt <u>dejected</u> when he did not make the baseball team.

   _____

FRIDAY • Writing Prompt

If you have a poem that is funny and just five lines long, it is likely a *limerick*.

The first, second, and fifth lines rhyme in this style of poem rhyme, and each line is eight syllables long or nine syllables long.

A limerick's third and fourth lines rhyme, and each line is either five syllables long or six syllables long.

These little poems are usually silly or about something funny. No one knows for sure where the name limerick comes from, but it may have something to do with the town of Limerick in Ireland.

Example: There was a young boy who one night
Decided a limerick to write.
It took him some time
To make it all rhyme
But finally he got it just right!

Write your own limerick.

☐ **Choose a subject for your limerick—something funny works well.**

☐ **Check that the first, second, and fifth lines rhyme.**

☐ **Ensure the first, second, and fifth lines are all eight or nine syllables long.**

☐ **Make sure the third and fourth lines rhyme with each other.**

☐ **Check that the third and fourth lines are both five or six syllables long.**

Line 1_____

Line 2_____

Line 3_____

Line 4_____

Line 5_____

MONDAY • Sentences and Punctuation

1. **What is missing in the sentence fragment below? Circle the answer.**

   The tranquil lake

   (who or what is doing   the action   the action both are missing)

2. **Rewrite the sentence fragment. Add what is missing to make a complete sentence.**

   _____

3. **Write the correct conjunction—_for_, _so_, or _yet_.**

   a) Rosa went to bed early _____ she would get a good night's sleep.

   b) Rick said he would call me today, _____ I haven't heard from him.

TUESDAY • Grammar and Usage

1. **Abstract nouns name ideas you cannot see or touch.**   _Example: pride_
   Underline the abstract nouns.

   Sometimes we feel anger when people tell us the truth about ourselves.

2. **Fill in the circle beside the sentence if the underlined pronoun has an unclear antecedent.**

   a) O Mrs. Tanaka removed the necklace from her jewellery box and sold <u>it</u>.

   b) O If the cars won't fit in the driveway, we can always make <u>it</u> wider.

3. **A phrase is a group of two or more words. A prepositional phrase begins with a preposition.**

   Example: The caption **under the photo** is very informative.
   Underline the prepositional phrase.

   The fruits and vegetables in this store look very fresh.

WEDNESDAY • Figures of Speech

1. **Read the sentence. Identify the figure of speech.**

   a) Tina said, "I was so nervous that I broke out in a cold sweat." _____

   b) Hail pounded the houses and streets. _____

   c) Freddy figured finding fudge would be fun and fulfilling. _____

2. **Write an example of a metaphor. Circle the two things being compared in the metaphor.**

   _____

3. **Use the oxymoron in a sentence to show its meaning.**

   thundering silence

   _____

THURSDAY • Vocabulary and Spelling

1. **Write the contraction for each pair of words.**

   a) has not _____ (hasn't hadn't)   **b)** must not _____ (mustn't must've)

2. **Underline the word or words that have a negative connotation.**

   a) paw through clothes   look through clothes

   b) glance at him   glare at him

3. **Fill in the blank with the correct word.**

   Have you _____ gone to the museum?   (all ready already)

4. **Write three words that belong in a group. Order them from general to specific.**

   Example: country   province   city

   _____

FRIDAY • Writing Prompt

A *proverb* is a saying that offers some advice on how to live your life.

1. a) Explain what you think the proverb below means. Draw the proverb.

"Necessity is the mother of invention."

_____

_____

b) Do you think the proverb relates to daily life or the world around you?

_____

_____

_____

_____

_____

☐ I checked for correct spelling. ☐ I organized my ideas in a way that makes sense.

☐ I checked for correct punctuation. ☐ I used linking words to connect my ideas.

☐ I used interesting words. ☐ Challenge: I used a figure of speech.

MONDAY • Sentences and Punctuation

1. Fill in the blank with the correct conjunction.

My friend likes to swim, _____ I prefer to go sailing.   (but   or)

2. Write a sentence for each sentence type.

Declarative: _____

Interrogative: _____

Imperative: _____

Exclamation: _____

3. Correct and rewrite the sentence.

Sophia is your address 16 oak place Halifax ns asked Mat

_____

TUESDAY • Grammar and Usage

1. Circle the antecedent of the underlined pronoun in each sentence.

a) We made lots of snacks for our guests, and we hope they enjoy <u>them</u>.

b) Since the sofa was too large to move in the car, we rented a van to move <u>it</u>.

2. Complete each sentence with the correct relative pronoun.

who   whom   whose   which   that

a) Mrs. Lee called the real estate agent _____ I had recommended.

b) We stayed at The Royal Hotel, _____ is the best hotel in the city.

3. Circle the prepositions in each sentence.

a) People threw coins into the fountain behind the hotel.

b) The fish at this restaurant comes from the Atlantic Ocean.

WEDNESDAY • Figures of Speech

1. Read the sentence. Identify the figure of speech.

a) Our principal said that recess was a zoo today. _____

b) My grandfather has a mind like a steel trap! _____

c) Lightning danced across the sky _____

2. Fill in the blanks with onomatopoeic words.

a) My dog's teeth _____ when it's really cold in the winter.

b) The stream _____ and _____ over the rocks.

3. Write an example of a simile.

_____

THURSDAY • Vocabulary and Spelling

1. The word in brackets is marked as a synonym (S), an antonym (A), or a homophone (H) for the missing word. Write the correct word in the blank.

a) It is said that an owl is a very _____ animal.   (foolish; **A**)

b) Havi _____ to the store to buy milk and eggs.   (strolled; **S**)

c) Our parents said we were _____ to go the movies with friends.   (aloud; **H**)

2. What is the meaning of the underlined word?

The school children generously raised money to <u>bestow</u> on the charity.

_____

FRIDAY • Writing Prompt

Would you rather travel back in time or into the future? Explain your thinking.

_____

_____

_____

_____

_____

_____

_____

_____

_____

_____

_____

_____

_____

_____

☐ I ordered my ideas in a way that makes sense.

☐ I checked for correct spelling and punctuation.

MONDAY • Sentences and Punctuation

1. Fill in the blank with the correct conjunction.

My mom listened to music _____ she cooked dinner.
(as soon as   while)

2. Read the sentence. Circle the complete subject. Underline the complete predicate.

Two of my pencil crayons need to be sharpened.

3. Write an example of a complex sentence.

_____

4. Write an imperative sentence that includes a speaker.

_____

TUESDAY • Grammar and Usage

1. Circle the correct pronoun in brackets for the antecedent in bold.

a) The television program was frequently interrupted by commercials from **sponsors** who wanted to sell (its their they're) products.

b) When we received the **email** from our grandparents, we were glad to see that (them they it) included several photos from their vacation.

2. Does the underlined linking verb link the subject to a noun or an adjective? Write "noun" or "adjective" beside each sentence.

a) Tickets for the concert <u>are</u> expensive. _____

b) These tadpoles will <u>become</u> frogs in two months. _____

3. Write a sentence that includes a proper noun, an adjective, and an adverb, and is in the past tense.

_____

WEDNESDAY • Figures of Speech

Match the figure of speech to its definition. Write the letter of the matching definition on the line.

1. alliteration _____

A. comparing two things that are not alike, but have something in common

2. metaphor _____

B. giving human qualities to an animal or an object

3. analogy _____

C. comparing two things by suggesting something is something else

4. simile _____

D. exaggerations used for emphasis and for humour

5. onomatopoeia _____

E. using the same sounds or letters several times in a sentence

6. hyperbole _____

F. using *like* or *as* to describe something or someone

7. personification _____

G. using a word that sounds like what it names

8. oxymoron _____

H. a pair of words that have opposite meanings

THURSDAY • Vocabulary and Spelling

1. The word in brackets is marked as a synonym (S), an antonym (A), or a homophone (H) for the missing word. Write the correct word in the blank.

a) After eating a good breakfast, Jim was full of _____ .   (power; **S**)

b) The lumberjacks _____ the huge tree down.   (sod; **H**)

c) The scientist was hoping to _____ a new species of dinosaur fossil.
(find; **S**)

2. Add a word that belongs to the group.

Toronto   Regina   Vancouver   _____

3. Correct and rewrite the sentence.

The fishes were swiming up stream.

_____

FRIDAY • Writing Prompt

What was the best advice you have ever been given? What was the outcome?

_____

_____

_____

_____

_____

_____

_____

_____

_____

_____

_____

_____

_____

_____

_____

☐ I checked for correct spelling. ☐ I organized my ideas in a way that makes sense.

☐ I checked for correct punctuation. ☐ I used linking words to connect my ideas.

☐ I used interesting words. ☐ Challenge: I used a figure of speech.

Student Writing Tips

Sentence Starters

Sentence starters for **stating your opinion** in a piece of writing:

In my opinion…	I think…	The best thing about…
I feel…	I prefer…	The worst thing about…
I believe…	I know…	_____ is better than _____

Sentence starters to use **when trying to persuade someone** in a piece of writing:

Of course…	Clearly…	The fact is…
Without doubt…	Everyone knows that…	It is clear that…

Transition Words

Transition words or phrases to use **when providing reasons** in a piece of writing:

First of all…	Next…	Most importantly…
Secondly…	Another reason…	To begin with…

Transition words or phrases to use **when providing examples** in a piece of writing:

For example…	In fact…	In addition…
For instance…	In particular…	Another example…

Transition words or phrases to **show cause and effect** in a piece of writing:

For this reason…	As a result…	Consequently…
Because of [fact]…	Therefore…	Due to [reason]…

Transition words to use **when comparing or contrasting** in a piece of writing:

Similarly…	But…	Although…
Like…	However…	Even though…

Transition words or phrases to use **when showing a sequence** in a piece of writing:

First…	Next…	After that…
Second…	Eventually…	Lastly…

Transition words or phrases to use **when concluding** a piece of writing:

Finally…	Lastly…	All in all…
In conclusion…	To sum up…	As you can see…

Canadian Daily Language Skills, Grade 6   © Chalkboard Publishing Inc.

Writing Planner

Ideas for My Paragraph

My Topic Sentence

What I Want to Say About the Topic

My Concluding Sentence

Adjectives for Writing

Category	Adjectives
Size	big, small, short, tall, fat, skinny, large, medium, slim, thin, slender, tiny, lean, scrawny, huge, gigantic, jumbo, plump, wee, wide, narrow
Shape	round, square, pointed, jagged, oval, chunky, curly, straight, curved, flat, twisted, heart-shaped, spiky, wavy, bent, tangled, messy
Colour	red, orange, yellow, green, blue, purple, pink, grey, white, black, brown, silver, gold
Age	young, old, new, baby, newborn
Sound	loud, quiet, long, short, musical, surprising, soft, noisy, muffled, whispering, growling, grumbling
Light and Brightness	dull, bright, dark, light, clear, flashy, flashing, dim, faint, glowing, flickering, twinkly, twinkling, shiny, shining
Smell	good, bad, strong, sweet, salty, spicy, stinky, sour, delicious, yummy, fresh, rotten, rotting
Feel and Texture	soft, hard, smooth, rough, silky, fluffy, fuzzy, furry, wet, dry, bumpy, lumpy, scratchy, sweaty, slippery, slimy, gritty, dirty, sticky, gummy, jiggly, wiggly, squishy, watery, liquid, solid, rock hard, damp, stiff, firm
Taste	delicious, bitter, sweet, salty, tasty, spicy, yummy, bland, sour, strong
Speed and Movement	quick, quickly, fast, slow, slowly, rapid, rapidly, brisk, briskly, swift, swiftly, instant, instantly
Temperature	hot, cold, icy, frosty, chilly, burning, boiling, steamy, sizzling, cool, warm, freezing, frozen, damp, humid, melting

Canadian Daily Language Skills, Grade 6   © Chalkboard Publishing Inc.

How Am I Doing?

	Completing my work	Using my time wisely	Following directions	Keeping organized
Full speed ahead!	• My work is always complete and done with care. • I added extra details to my work.	• I always get my work done on time.	• I always follow directions.	• My materials are always neatly organized. • I am always prepared and ready to learn.
Keep going!	• My work is complete and done with care. • I added extra details to my work.	• I usually get my work done on time.	• I usually follow directions without reminders.	• I usually can find my materials. • I am usually prepared and ready to learn.
Slow down!	• My work is complete. • I need to check my work.	• I sometimes get my work done on time.	• I sometimes need reminders to follow directions.	• I sometimes need time to find my materials. • I am sometimes prepared and ready to learn.
Stop!	• My work is not complete. • I need to check my work.	• I rarely get my work done on time.	• I need reminders to follow directions.	• I need to organize my materials. • I am rarely prepared and ready to learn.

_____'s _Completion Chart_

Week	Monday	Tuesday	Wednesday	Thursday	Friday
1					
2					
3					
4					
5					
6					
7					
8					
9					
10					
11					
12					
13					
14					
15					
16					
17					
18					
19					
20					
21					
22					
23					
24					
25					
26					
27					
28					
29					
30					
31					
32					
33					
34					
35					

Canadian Daily Language Skills, Grade 6   © Chalkboard Publishing Inc.

Achievement Award

Fantastic Work!

Canadian Daily Language Skills, Grade 6

Answers to Exercises

WEEK 1, pp. 3–5

Monday   1. Complete Sentence We need to go to the store. **Sentence Fragment** Going to the store.
2. Complete Subject a) The green garden snake b) The new couch in the family room   **3. Complete Predicate** a) tumbled and twirled in the wind. b) chased after the blue and white ball.
Tuesday   1. Common Nouns tourists, city **Proper Nouns** Rome, Italy   **2.** I   **3.** a) have b) is
Wednesday   1. Literal; Figurative   **2.** a) Ingrid is an innovator inspired by intelligent individuals. b) Five fabulous flamingos finished eating their favourite food.
3. green
Thursday   1. a) afford b) mature c) comfort d) collect
2. a) permit b) divide   **3.** a) natural b) rare
Friday   Answers will vary. Ensure the child has covered the items in, and marked off, the checklist at the bottom of the exercise.

WEEK 2, pp. 6–8

Monday   1. a) period; command b) question mark; question c) period; statement c) exclamation mark; exclamation   **2.** for
Tuesday   1. teams'   **2.** a) **Transitive Verb** brushes **Direct Object** teeth b) **Transitive Verb** showed **Direct Object** photos   **3.** a) beside, in b) between, along
Wednesday   1. Come clean your cluttered closet.
2. Answers will vary. Ensure the sentence includes a repetition of sounds   **3.** a) yes; like a fish out of water b) no
Thursday   1. a) flower b) flour   **2.** knapsack = k, k; thumb = b; gnome = g, e; wrist = w; knot = k
3. farther   **4.** Answers will vary. Sample answer: soft
Friday   Answers will vary. Ensure the child has covered the items in, and marked off, the checklist at the bottom of the exercise.

WEEK 3, pp. 9–11

Monday   1. Answers will vary. Ensure each sentence has a subject and a verb that agree, and ends with the correct punctuation mark.   **2.** yet   **3.** My grandfather's birthday is July 7, 1945.
Tuesday   1. a) Aunt Mary b) Kevin   **2.** a) Could b) should

Wednesday   1. jumped twenty metres
2. Answers will vary. Ensure the sentence includes an exaggeration.   **3.** a) like a fish out of water b) Answers will vary. Sample answer: Gary felt he did not belong.
Thursday   1. a) Mon. b) Dec. c) Rd.   **2.** two, to
3. a) boxes b) dishes c) bunches   **4.** aircraft, lifetime, fireplace, anybody
Friday   Answers will vary. Ensure the child has covered the items in, and marked off, the checklist at the bottom of the exercise.

WEEK 4, pp. 12–14

Monday   1. a) compound b) complex
Tuesday   1. a) scientist's b) workers   **2.** a) whose b) that   **3.** a) This b) these
Wednesday   1. a) Sam, rat b) backyard, lake
2. Answers will vary.
Thursday   1. a) I've b) you've   **2.** ability
3. a) adjusted **or** adjustable b) playful
Friday   Answers will vary. Ensure the child has covered the items in, and marked off, the checklist at the bottom of the exercise.

WEEK 5, pp. 15–17

Monday   1. a) The waiter asked, "Would you like more water?" b) My sister complained, "That's not fair!"   **2.** a) question mark; question b) period; command
Tuesday   1. Common Nouns patient, ambulance **Proper Nouns** City Centre Hospital; Dr. Patel
2. a) across, at b) into, behind   **3.** a) **Adverb** later **Verb** leave b) **Adverb** away **Verb** ran   **4.** girls'
Wednesday   1. Answers will vary. Ensure the sentence includes a repetition of sounds.   **2.** Answers will vary. Ensure the sentence includes **as** or **like**.
3. a river of tears   **4.** a) up b) hot   **5.** Answers will vary. Ensure the sentence uses an exaggeration.
Thursday   1. a) began b) extra   **2.** a) flies b) valleys c) babies d) toys   **3.** Answers will vary. Sample answer: a) He took a bow at the end of the concert. b) She tied her hair back with a bow.
Friday   Answers will vary. Ensure the first letters spell a word when read vertically.

   Canadian Daily Language Skills, Grade 6   © Chalkboard Publishing Inc.

WEEK 6, pp. 18–20

Monday 1. a) "It's time to go home," said Mrs. Jackson. b) "I think you're amazing!" Rob told Jamal.
2. a) Yes, I followed the cookie recipe, but I also added some chocolate chips. a) No, I prefer to walk to the store.
Tuesday 1. a) I b) me 2. a) **Transitive Verb** sing **Direct Object** songs b) **Transitive Verb** bought **Direct Object** supplies
Wednesday 1. a) dull roar 2. Answers will vary. 3. life, dream
Thursday 1. a) synonyms b) antonyms 2. a) pianos b) echoes c) potatoes 3. good 4. Answers will vary. Sample answer: Paul got a new front tire on his bike.
Friday Answers will vary. Ensure the child has covered the items in, and marked off, the checklist at the bottom of the exercise.

WEEK 7, pp. 21–23

Monday 1. a) "This clue," said the detective, "is very interesting." b) "Your conclusion," said the teacher, "is based on strong evidence." 2. a) The weather is cold for May, isn't it? b) Our class has music after lunch, don't we?
Tuesday 1. bird's 2. b) I **am** late for hockey practice. 3. Answers will vary.
Wednesday 1. belch, clunk, giggle, hum, screech, oink 2. Answers will vary. Ensure the sentence includes a word that sounds like what it names. 3. Answers will vary. Ensure the sentence includes a repetition of sounds. 4. dying to go
Thursday 1. fudge = e; rhombic = h; scenic = c
2. too, to 3. a) wives b) cliffs c) shelves 4. Two people waited patiently to share their concerns with the principal.
Friday Answers will vary. Ensure the child has covered the items in, and marked off, the checklist at the bottom of the exercise.

WEEK 8, pp. 24–26

Monday 1. a) "Angela, could you please help me fold the laundry?" Mom asked. b) The children said, "You made a great dinner tonight, Dad." 2. a) "I'll give you one more chance," the boss told Henry. b) "Why did I do that?" I asked myself. 3. **Complete Subject** Fluffy white clouds **Complete Predicate** drifted across the sky.
Tuesday 1. audience 2. a) whom b) who 3. will
Wednesday 1. a) lightning b) danced c) Answers will vary. Sample answer: People, not lightning, dance.

2. a) desert, heaven b) Answers will vary. Ensure the metaphor does not use **as** or **like**.
Thursday 1. a) patients b) patience 2. a) they'll b) we'd 3. a) woods b) ratios c) men 4. five 5. petrified
Friday Answers will vary. Ensure the child has covered the items in, and marked off, the checklist at the bottom of the exercise.

WEEK 9, pp. 27–29

Monday 1. a) "Alexa, you need to get ready for your appointment," Mom said. b) "Maybe you could come too, Carlos," I suggested. 2. For lunch we had burritos, vegetable sticks, and milk. 3. Answers will vary.
Tuesday 1. book's 2. a) I b) me 3. a) My grandfather **was** a plumber.
Wednesday 1. a) taxi cab b) was impatient c) Answers will vary. Sample answer: People, not cars, grow impatient. 2. honk, rattle, peep, clank, moo, whine, smack 3. Answers will vary. 4. a) drink b) drive
Thursday 1. a) Sat. b) Tues. c) Fri. 2. a) country, nation; S b) past, present; A c) hour, our; H 3. a) accept b) except 4. Aren't these red strawberries delicious?
Friday Answers will vary. The child should have reasons for his or her argument.

WEEK 10, pp. 30–32

Monday 1. CP 2. a) "Please feel free to ask questions," said the guest speaker. b) "When will the train leave?" the young woman asked. 3. Jupiter, Saturn, and Uranus are the largest planets in our solar system. 4. complex
Tuesday 1. **Common Nouns** tickets, shows **Proper Nouns** Winchester Theatre; Mondays. 2. **Transitive Verb** caught **Direct Object** puck 3. was
Wednesday 1. **Idiom** chew someone out **Meaning** yell at someone **Idiom** down to the wire **Meaning** rushing to meet a deadline **Idiom** finger lickin' good **Meaning** delicious **Idiom** when pigs fly **Meaning** never will happen 2. Answers may vary. Sample answers: a) slurped b) crunched 3. Answers will vary.
Thursday 1. **Long a** integration, fair, dare, always, table **Short a** actual, absolutely 2. a) flies b) valleys c) blackberries d) babies) toys e) decoys 3. deer 4. four 5. clearly visible
Friday Answers will vary. Ensure the child has covered the items in, and marked off, the checklist at the bottom of the exercise.

WEEK 11, pp. 33–35

Monday **1.** period; statement **2. Complete Subject** A brown squirrel **Complete Predicate** ran along the fence. **3.** but **4.** a) "It's a good plan," agreed Paul, "but will it work?" b) I think Angelo plays on the soccer team, doesn't he?

Tuesday **1.** a) printer's b) TV's **2.** who **3.** on, for **4.** very, quickly

Wednesday **1.** Answers will vary. **2.** a) nest b) arm **3.** a) unbiased opinion b) big baby **4.** Answers will vary.

Thursday **1.** bad **2.** a) antonyms b) synonyms **3.** a) all ready b) its **4.** Answers may vary. Sample answers: beg, plead with

Friday Answers will vary. Ensure the poems follow the format of two syllables, four syllables, six syllables, eight syllables, two syllables.

WEEK 12, pp. 36–38

Monday **1.** There are several items on my shopping list: eggs, milk, bread, tea, and juice. **2.** a) Yes, I am coming back later. b) The volleyball game is at 2 o'clock, isn't it? **3.** a) Minnie exclaimed, "I didn't know your dog was having puppies!" b) Mrs. Stevens said in a welcoming voice, "John, please make yourself at home." **4.** so

Tuesday **1. Common Nouns** year, weather, month **Proper Nouns** April, Uncle Max. **2.** a) me b) I **3.** The woman's perfume **smelled** nice.

Wednesday **1.** Answers will vary. **2.** Answers will vary. Ensure the sentence uses an exaggeration.

Thursday **1.** a) their b) they're c) There **2.** Answers will vary. Sample answers: main, cane, train, gain, lane **3.** Mr. Tanaka can't attend the meeting being held at 25 Beech St.

Friday Answers will vary. Ensure the child has covered the items in, and marked off, the checklist at the bottom of the exercise.

WEEK 13, pp. 39–41

Monday **1.** The store had three flavours of yogurt: strawberry, blueberry, and vanilla. **2.** who or what is doing the action **3.** Answers will vary. Ensure the complete sentence has a subject and a verb that agree. **4.** Answers will vary. Ensure the sentence includes quotation marks and ends with an exclamation mark .

Tuesday **1.** My partner and I **2.** a) **Transitive Verb** boils **Direct Object** water b) **Transitive Verb** delivers **Direct Object** parcels **3.** would **4.** a) ADJ b) N

Wednesday **1.** a) Canada; melting pot b) José, worm **2.** Answers will vary. Ensure each sentence uses an exaggeration. **3.** a) hope b) walked c) Answers will vary. Sample answer: Only people or animals walk.

Thursday **1.** Answers will vary. Sample answers: came out, appeared, came forth, came out of **2.** cologne = e, g; knight = k, g, h; rhythm = h **3.** Answers may vary. Sample answer: refused **4.** neither, nor

Friday Answers will vary. Ensure the child has covered the items in, and marked off, the checklist at the bottom of the exercise.

WEEK 14, pp. 42–44

Monday **1.** nor **2.** compound **3.** "Don't go outside in the rain!" **4.** Dinosaur Provincial Park in Drumheller, Alberta, is a popular tourist attraction.

Tuesday **1. Common Nouns** people, display, fireworks **Proper Nouns** Parliament Hill; Ottawa **2.** their **3.** whose **4.** along the highway

Wednesday **1.** Answers will vary. **2.** month **3.** Answers will vary. **4.** a) as nimble as a monkey b) Answers will vary. Sample answer: agile, spry, acrobatic

Thursday **1.** demolished **2.** a) altar b) alter **3.** a) they'd b) we've **4.** warned

Friday Answers will vary. Ensure the child has covered the items in, and marked off, the checklist at the bottom of the exercise.

WEEK 15, pp. 45–47

Monday **1.** compound **2.** These are the people on my team: Wyatt, Owen, Sydney, and Andrew. **3.** "If you're busy," said Rachel, "I could call you later." **4.** question mark; question **5.** Answers will vary. Ensure the sentence has a subject and a verb that agree, and ends with a period.

Tuesday **1. Sophia** gave **Mom her** gloves. **Mom** passed **her** gloves to Sophia. **2.** a) paintings b) dog's **3.** is **4.** That

Wednesday **1.** a) yes b) yes c) no **2.** a) no b) yes **3.** a hundred years old!

Thursday **1.** isn't **2.** Fewer **3.** triathlon **4.** Answers may vary. Sample answers: often, regularly

Friday Answers will vary. Ensure the child has covered the items in, and marked off, the checklist at the bottom of the exercise.

Canadian Daily Language Skills, Grade 6   © Chalkboard Publishing Inc.

WEEK 16, pp. 48–50

Monday   1. Complete Subject The passengers on the train **Complete Predicate** showed their tickets to the conductor.   **2.** complex   **3.** "What a wonderful gift!" exclaimed Roberto.   **4.** yes   **5.** Answers will vary. Ensure the sentence ends with a question mark.
Tuesday   1. kindness   **2.** me   **3.** a) adjective b) noun
Wednesday   1. zip, zap, zoom   **2.** Answers will vary. Ensure the sentence includes words that sound like what they name.   **3.** a) rain b) giving pecks on the cheek c) Answers will vary. Sample answer: Rain cannot give pecks.   **4.** Answers will vary. The sentence should use one of: alliteration, metaphor, analogy, simile, onomatopoeia, hyperbole, personification, or oxymoron.
Thursday   1. scent   **2.** a) I'd b) you've
3. a) sandwiches b) burritos d) mouses c) oxen d) mice   **4.** Answers will vary. Sample answer: weakening
Friday   Answers will vary. Ensure the child follows the format of a Diamond poem using nouns, verbs, and adjectives.

WEEK 17, pp. 51–53

Monday   1. CS   **2.** when   **3.** "When I was a little girl," said Grandma, "we walked a mile to school every day."   **4.** exclamation mark; command
Tuesday   1. a) its b) they   **2.** a) **Transitive Verb** checks **Direct Object** answers   b) **Transitive Verb** inserted **Direct Object** paper   **3.** a) through, with b) in, beside
Wednesday   1. a) Answers will vary. Sample answers: a) an owl b) a door; a floorboard; a stair
2. Answers will vary.   **3.** a) eats like a bird b) Answers will vary. Sample answer: has been around forever
4. Answers will vary. Ensure the sentence includes a repetition of sounds.
Thursday   1. a) she'd b) he'll   **2.** Answers will vary. Ensure the word has three syllables.   **3.** write, right
4. neither, nor   **5.** food, dessert, cake
Friday   Answers will vary. Ensure the child has covered the items in, and marked off, the checklist at the bottom of the exercise.

WEEK 18, pp. 54–56

Monday   1. who or what is doing the action
2. Answers will vary. Ensure the complete sentence has a subject and a verb that agree.   **3.** yet
4. "We've eaten at this restaurant before, haven't we?" asked Leo.

Tuesday   1. Tina   **2.** who   **3.** should **or** will
Wednesday   1. a) buckle down b) Answers will vary.
2. a) yes b) no   **3.** toes   **4.** Answers will vary. Ensure the sentence uses an exaggeration.
Thursday   1. a) ea b) ey c) ee d) ie   **2.** chefs
3. There are ten families who live on our street.
Friday   Answers will vary. Ensure the child has covered the items in, and marked off, the checklist at the bottom of the exercise.

WEEK 19, pp. . 57–59

Monday   1. nor   **2.** "May I help you?" asked the salesperson.   **3.** compound   **4.** I am going!
5. Answers will vary.
Tuesday   1. I provided **reasons** for my **conclusions**, but **they** aren't very clear. **Mrs. Shultz** told **her neighbour** that **her** dog got out of the yard.   **2.** me
3. a) has b) have
Wednesday   1. a) close distance b) Answers will vary   **2.** toes; ice cubes   **3.** Answers will vary. Ensure the sentence includes words that sound like what they name.   **4.** Answers will vary. Ensure the sentence uses an exaggeration.
Thursday   1. a) Ave. b) Mr. c) Que.   **2.** a) beginning, conclusion; A b) pail, pale; H   **3.** really   **4.** Answers will vary. Ensure the word has four syllables.
Friday   Answers will vary. Ensure the child has covered the items in, and marked off, the checklist at the bottom of the exercise.

WEEK 20, pp. 60–62

Monday   1. Complete Subject The house with the black roof **Complete Predicate**   caught fire last week.   **2.** exclamation mark; exclamation   **3.** The animals at the zoo include: mammals, reptiles, birds, and amphibians.   **4.** I can't wait to visit Stanley Park in Vancouver, British Columbia!
Tuesday   1. Common Nouns mayor, questions, reporters **Proper Nouns** Friday; City Hall   **2.** them
3. adjective
Wednesday   1. Answers will vary.   **2.** a) sizzling, onomatopoeia b) jumped, personification
3. a) temper, volcano b) bedroom, zoo
Thursday   1. rhapsody = h; wedge = e; enough = o
2. Answers will vary. The child should choose one of the following: Jan. Feb. Mar. Apr. May June July Aug. Sept. Oct. Nov. Dec.   **3.** a) I've; I have b) They're; They are   **4.** a) people b) trout
Friday   Answers will vary. Ensure the child has covered the items in, and marked off, the checklist at the bottom of the exercise.

WEEK 21, pp. 63–65

Monday **1.** a) so b) but **2.** "I have the flu," explained Kim, "so I can't come." **3.** This is the best pizza I have ever eaten! **4.** Riding a bike, walking to school, and playing sports are all good exercise.
Tuesday **1.** **Mr. Lee** told **his nephew** that **he** had artistic talent. **2.** a) **Transitive Verb** broke **Direct Object** large branch b) **Transitive Verb** cook **Direct Object** steaks **3.** a) N b) ADJ
Wednesday **1.** Answers will vary. **2.** clanging, onomatopoeia; woke up the whole city, personification **3.** a) opportunity, knocking b) Answers will vary. **4.** Answers will vary.
Thursday **1.** more **2.** a) she'll b) he'd **3.** a) ti b) ci c) ti **4.** Answers will vary. Sample answer: starving **5.** Answers will vary. Ensure the word has four syllables.
Friday Answers will vary. Ensure the child has covered the items in, and marked off, the checklist at the bottom of the exercise.

WEEK 22, pp. 66–68

Monday **1.** no **2.** "I am very proud of you, Sophia," said Grandma, "I can see you have worked hard." **3.** Answers will vary. Ensure each clause has a subject and predicate. **4.** My friends and I shared some milk, cookies, and apple slices.
Tuesday **1.** students, they **2.** politician's **3.** a) can b) will **4.** whose
Wednesday **1.** a) turkey dinner b) didn't agree c) Answers will vary. Ensure the sentence includes words that sound like what they name. **2.** Answers will vary. Ensure the sentence includes a word that sounds like what it names. **3.** Answers will vary. Ensure the sentence includes a repetition of sounds.
Thursday **1.** a) wolves b) burritos **2.** a) couldn't b) wouldn't **3.** Answers may vary. Sample answer: mistake **4.** a) busiest b) stopped
Friday Answers will vary. Ensure the child has covered the items in, and marked off, the checklist at the bottom of the exercise.

WEEK 23, pp. 69–71

Monday **1.** as soon as **2.** The child whispered, "I know the answer to the secret." **3.** who or what is doing the action **4.** Answers will vary. Ensure the complete sentence has a subject and a verb that agree.
Tuesday **1.** patriotism, freedom **2.** a) whom b) which **3.** a) stop b) has

Wednesday **1.** Answers will vary. **2.** a) glove b) narrow **3.** Answers will vary. Ensure the sentence uses an exaggeration. **4.** day screeched to a halt; personification
Thursday **1.** a) fragile, delicate; S b) creek, creak: H **2.** a) she'll b) he'd **3.** most **4.** I saw some beautiful butterflies flying around the patios.
Friday Answers will vary. Ensure the child has covered the items in, and marked off, the checklist at the bottom of the exercise.

WEEK 24, pp. 72–74

Monday **1.** **Complete Subject** The loud construction outside **Complete Predicate** woke me up early this morning. **2.** period; statement **3.** for **4.** "Felix, go to Mexican Delight and pick up tortilla chips, salsa, and burritos," said Dad.
Tuesday **1.** it **2.** me **3.** The crumbling old bridge **seemed** unsafe.
Wednesday **1.** Answers will vary. Ensure the sentence includes a repetition of sounds and the word **as** or **like**. **2.** a) as clear as mud b) Answers will vary. **3.** a) complained; personification b) noisy, quiet; analogy c) monster snow cone; hyperbole
Thursday **1.** a) Jan. b) l **or** L c) tbsp. **or** Tbsp. **2.** Answers will vary. Sample answer: lacking **3.** a) ci b) ti c) ci **4.** oldest
Friday Answers will vary. Ensure the child has covered the items in, and marked off, the checklist at the bottom of the exercise.

WEEK 25, pp. . 75–77

Monday **1.** Answers will vary. Ensure the sentence has one main clause and at least one subordinate clause. **2.** "Get out of my way!" yelled the driver, "I'm in a hurry!" **3.** yet **4.** Glen, is it true that St. Patrick's Day is Morgan's favourite holiday?
Tuesday **1.** Take the **radio** out of the **box** and then give **it** to me. **2.** noun **3.** about, by
Wednesday **1.** a) dreams b) died c) Answers will vary. **2.** Answers will vary. **3.** Answers will vary. **4.** chili, fireworks; hyperbole
Thursday **1.** **Long i** island, dice high **Short i** impress, majority, listen **2.** a) antonym b) homophone c) antonym d) synonym **3.** Answers may vary. Sample answers: a) refused b) rare
Friday Answers will vary. Ensure the child has covered the items in, and marked off, the checklist at the bottom of the exercise.

WEEK 26, pp. 78–80

Monday   1. a) √   **2.** a) The waiter asked, "Would you like more water?" b) "Please hand in your papers," said the teacher.   **3.** Who knows where the car is parked!
Tuesday   1. carpets   **2.** a) **Transitive Verb** balanced **Direct Object** a ball b) **Transitive Verb** carries **Direct Object** the suitcases   **3.** by the lake
Wednesday   1. Answers will vary.   **2.** Answers will vary. Ensure the sentence includes a repetition of sounds.   **3.** a) world, stage b) Answers will vary.
Thursday   1. receipt = i, p; assign = s, g; climb = b   **2.** a) isn't b) it's   **3.** a) bodies b) mosses c) hunches   **4.** a) synonym b) homophone c) antonym   **5.** worst
Friday   Answers will vary. Ensure the child has covered the items in, and marked off, the checklist at the bottom of the exercise.

WEEK 27, pp. 81–83

Monday   1. a) CS b) CP   **2.** exclamation mark **or** period; exclamation **or** statement   **3.** "For this weather," said Dad, "you need a warm coat."   **4.** so
Tuesday   1. a) fire, it b) students, they   **2.** a) whose b) whom   **3.** might
Wednesday   1. crash and clatter; onomatopoeia b) analogy   **2.** Answers will vary. Ensure the sentence uses an exaggeration.   **3.** Answers will vary.
Thursday   1. aren't   **2.** happiest   **3.** bad, worse
4. Answers will vary. Sample answer: difficulty
Friday   Answers will vary. Ensure the child has covered the items in, and marked off, the checklist at the bottom of the exercise.

WEEK 28, pp. 84–86

Monday   1. "Raj ate lunch with his sister," said Tobi, "and I ate with Sanjay."   **2. Complete Subject** That part of the movie **Complete Predicate** was so funny that I laughed out loud.   **3.** since   **4.** who or what is doing the action
Tuesday   1. compassion   **2.** If you have **questions** for the **guest speakers**, you should ask **them**.
3. was
Wednesday   1. a) frost, painted; personification b) room, disaster area; hyperbole   **2.** Answers will vary. Ensure the sentence includes words that sound like what they name.   **3. Alliteration** Answers will vary. Ensure the sentence includes a repetition of sounds.
4. Answers will vary.

Thursday   1. a) can't b) won't   **2.** best   **3.** a) houses b) choruses   **4.** Answers will vary. Sample answer: missing
Friday   Answers will vary. Ensure the poems follow the format of five syllables, seven syllables, five syllables.

WEEK 29, pp. 87–89

Monday   1. period; statement   **2.** compound   **3.** "I don't understand this math!" exclaimed Carlos, "Can you please help me?"   **4.** CP
Tuesday   1. a) their b) it   **2.** Scientists **are** fascinated by this new species of frog.   **3.** under the shady tree
Wednesday   1. a) proud as a peacock; simile b) happy mood, died; personification   **2.** Answers will vary. Ensure the sentence uses an exaggeration.
3. Answers will vary.   **4.** Answers will vary. Ensure the sentence includes **as** or **like**.
Thursday   1. There   **2.** dew, feet   **3.** a) windows b) mixes c) batteries   **4.** a) hasn't b) mustn't
5. some; any
Friday   Answers will vary. Ensure the child has covered the items in, and marked off, the checklist at the bottom of the exercise.

WEEK 30, pp. 90–92

Monday   1. or   **2.** The teacher gave us each some paper, a pencil, and an eraser for the test.   **3.** Dave asked, "Did you find the book you were looking for, Jayce?"   **4.** Answers will vary. Ensure each clause has a subject and predicate.
Tuesday   1. If you're too warm with a **sweater** under your **coat**, take **it** off.   **Joan** told **Helen** that no one would believe **her**.   **2.** a) from, to b) between, on
3. a) N b) ADJ
Wednesday   1. a) a million years; hyperbole b) alliteration c) constant change; oxymoron
2. Alliteration Answers will vary. Ensure the sentence includes a repetition of sounds.   **3.** Answers will vary.
Thursday   1. pale   **2. Long o** known, fold, rolling, most, toast, modal **Short o** dolphin, smog, got
3. a) don't b) won't   **4.** more
Friday   Answers will vary. Ensure the child has covered the items in, and marked off, the checklist at the bottom of the exercise.

WEEK 31, pp. 93–95

Monday   1. Complete Subject The pilot **Complete Predicate** flew the plane right across three provinces.   **2.** because   **3.** Gigi and her family live

in Charlottetown, Prince Edward Island.   **4.** I said, "We're going to the mall, Mia," but we're really taking her to the zoo.
Tuesday   1. a) me b) me   **2.** a) **Transitive Verb** pressed **Direct Object** button b) **Transitive Verb** painted **Direct Object** fence   **3.** adverb
Wednesday   1. Answers will vary.   **2.** a) rumbled like thunder b) Answers will vary.   **3.** a) avalanche devoured; personification
Thursday   1. two, to   **2.** a) control b) correct
3. a) lessen b) lesson   **4.** paragraph, sentence, word
Friday   Answers will vary. Ensure the child has covered the items in, and marked off, the checklist at the bottom of the exercise.

WEEK 32, pp. 96–98

Monday   1. exclamation mark; exclamation
2. Judy whined, "Dad said I have to clean my room this weekend!"   **3.** The dog chased the squirrel, **and** the squirrel ran away. **or** The dog chased the squirrel, **but** the squirrel ran away.   **4.** Answers will vary. Ensure items in the series are separated by commas, and that the sentence ends with a question mark.
Tuesday   1. its b) their   **2.** a) may b) can   **3.** a) have b) wants
Wednesday   1. Answers will vary.   **2.** a) a new classic; oxymoron b) flew off the shelves; personification   **3.** Answers will vary. Ensure the sentence includes a repetition of sounds and a phrase with the word **as** or **like**.   **4.** Answers will vary. Ensure the sentence uses an exaggeration.
Thursday   1. a) stores b) flamingos   **2.** a) doesn't b) aren't   **3.** heard, herd; H   **4.** Answers will vary. Sample answers: depressed, dispirited
Friday   Answers will vary. Ensure the poem follows the format of a limerick.

WEEK 33, pp. 99–101

Monday   1. the action   **2.** Answers will vary. Ensure the complete sentence has a subject and a verb that agree.   3. a) so b) but
Tuesday   1. anger, truth   **2.** Mrs. Tanaka removed **the necklace** from her **jewellery box** and sold **it**.
3. in this store
Wednesday   1. a) cold sweat; oxymoron b) Hail pounded; personification c) alliteration   **2.** Answers will vary. Ensure the metaphor does not use **as** or **like**.   **3.**   **4.** Answers will vary.
Thursday   1. a) hasn't b) mustn't   **2.** a) paw through clothes b) glare at him   **3.** already   **4.** Answers will

vary. Ensure the words follow the order of largest to smallest (general to specific).
Friday   Answers will vary. Ensure the child has covered the items in, and marked off, the checklist at the bottom of the exercise.

WEEK 34, pp. 102–104

Monday   1. but   **2.** Answers will vary. Ensure each sentence has a subject and a verb that agree, and ends with the correct punctuation mark.   **3.** "Sophia, is your address 16 Oak Place, Halifax, NS?" asked Matt.
Tuesday   1. a) snacks **or** lots of snacks b) sofa
2. a) whom b) which   **3.** a) into, behind b) at, from
Wednesday   1. a) recess, zoo; hyperbole b) mind like a steel trap; simile c) lightning danced; personification   **2.** Answers will vary. Sample answers: a) chatter b) burbled and chuckled
3. Answers will vary. Ensure the sentence includes **as** or **like**.
Thursday   1. a) wise b) walked c) allowed
2. Answers will vary. Sample answers: present (to), award, confer (on)
Friday   Answers will vary. Ensure the child has covered the items in, and marked off, the checklist at the bottom of the exercise.

WEEK 35, pp. 105–107

Monday   1. while   **2. Complete Subject** Two of my pencil crayons **Complete Predicate** need to be sharpened.   **3.** Answers will vary. Ensure the sentence has one main clause and at least one subordinate clause.   **4.** Answers will vary. Ensure the sentence tells someone to do something, ends with a period or exclamation mark, and includes quotation marks.
Tuesday   1. a) their b) it   **2.** a) adjective b) noun
3. Answers will vary.
Wednesday   1. alliteration = E   **2.** metaphor = C
3. analogy = A   **4.** simile = F   **5.** onomatopoeia = G
6. hyperbole = D   **7.** personification = B   **8.** oxymoron = H
Thursday   1. a) energy b) sawed c) discover
2. Answers will vary. Ensure the word names a Canadian city.   **3.** The fish were swimming upstream.
Friday   Answers will vary. Ensure the child has covered the items in, and marked off, the checklist at the bottom of the exercise.

   Canadian Daily Language Skills, Grade 6   © Chalkboard Publishing Inc.